Not a Blueprint:
It's the Shoe Prints
that Matter

A Journey Through Toxic Relationships

By Nina Norstrom

Georgia

Published in the United States by WriteLife Publishing
www.writelife.com
Printed in the United States of America

978-1-939371-47-8 (p)
978-1-939371-48-5 (e)

Library of Congress Control Number: 2014953324

Book design by Robin Krauss, www.bookformatters.com
Cover design by Dave Grauel, www.davidgrauel.com

A Tribute

There was this Angel, a very young, sweet, beautiful, caring, and special person. Surely she'd dropped from our heavenly skies above, but couldn't stay very long.

In her time spent here, she touched my life and those of others. When she came to be with me, she showered everyone who knew her with her precious gifts.

Teaching was one of the specialties she cherished—this I knew, 'cause she taught me about life: about caring, commitment, courage, dedication, strength, and mastering the everyday ups and downs. I learned a great deal from her. She was an awesome teacher, a specialist in her field.

Even though I only had the chance to know her for a short while, it was *her* life I was chosen to share. And out of all the people on this Earth, I was the one God handpicked to embrace her existence. So—I dedicate this book to her. Until our paths cross again, keep with you all my LOVE—my little Angel.

I also dedicate this book to all the children of the world—children everywhere who have experienced or may experience a toxic relationship.

Gratitude

Most importantly, I'd like to acknowledge God. It was He, our Holy Father, who gave me breath to inhale a new life. In this relationship, He's the owner of my being and the leader who guided me through my fiery journey. Yes, I've been to hell and made it back. But without His blessings, I wouldn't have escaped the burning inferno. Now, I'm in a better place physically, mentally, and emotionally. And for that, I praise His name.

Friends and Professional Groups

A special thanks! I've not forgotten my supporters who guided me through my recovery stage. Since there were so many, the list is endless. Please know that *each of you* was instrumental in this role. Your efforts made it possible. It was your presence and unconditional love that provided the mechanisms needed to shine the light to recovery.

Many years have passed from when I started my first manuscript, as a journal. Completing this work has been a major task, one I could not have conquered without the guidance you've given. The art of your skill was truly an asset in the completion of this book.

So, thanks to all for what you've done! You mean so much—and for that, I'm grateful.

Publisher and Editor

I have an abundance of appreciation for Terri Leidich, President/Publisher of WriteLife Publishing. She knows so well the emotional relationship one endures from the loss of a child. Thanks, Terri, for taking an interest in my work! A special warm thank-you to my editor and project manager for believing in me, being patient with my rewrites, and giving structure to the story. I shall always remember how you've helped me break through this writing journey. Also, gratitude to the cover designer, proofreaders, and other team members at WriteLife Publishing. Absolutely, everyone's expertise and professionalism assisted greatly in the presentation of it all. Such a wonderful group to have worked with! Thank you all for taking a chance on me.

Readers

I'm exceptionally appreciative to the readers who have shown interest in my work. Hopefully, you will enjoy this story and agree that its reading heightened your awareness and knowledge. There is no life without a relationship of some form or another. To breathe brings on a relationship with life. And when touched by a disease, its manifestation gives us a relationship with toxic invaders. No parent or child should have to endure a battle without the ammunition to strike back. Your support in purchasing this book will help gain an edge in the fight against toxic relationships.

Contents at a Glance

Author's Note

God be the glory . . . for walking me through the journey!

We are living in turbulent days, and our culture is clouded with a mass of toxicity. During our lifetimes, every one of us experiences some form of toxic relationship. These relationships aren't necessarily with people. We can have toxic relationships with alcohol, animals, battlefields, diseases, drugs, environments, religions, and even our own emotions. A toxic relationship, in any form, can destroy us physically, mentally, emotionally, and spiritually. But it can also offer us the opportunity to learn and grow. This is my story of those lessons learned and the shoe prints they have left on my life.

I've been a daughter, sister, mother, friend, worker, wife, and mistress. Lord knows, I've had my fair share of toxicity. My relationships with toxic people, diseases, emotions, religions, and work environments internally destroyed me.

There is no doubt toxicity trails us no matter what paths we take. Regardless of toxic relationships, my belief is that God gives us strong shoes to walk those paths. If we are willing, we can readily learn to distinguish whether relationships are toxic or nontoxic. My ultimate lesson in my journey has been that healthy relationships require honesty, compassion, strength, and courage. Given the right mechanisms, these traits make maneuvering through life less stormy.

Follow my shoe prints . . . the trail unfolds inside these pages.

Reminiscences of Life

On March 24, 1971, I bore into this life a little baby girl. I watched the cycle blossom as she began embracing each development—*babyhood, childhood, and adulthood.* As a mother, I didn't have much to provide. Yet, I gave her that which was given to me: *love, joy, happiness, and pain.*

We struggled endlessly to stay above the water. The journey we traveled took us across rough roads, around in circles, up steep hills, down deep valleys, and through high mountain chains. And with her strapped over my shoulders, I'd thought she'd be mine to keep. Maybe it was a fantasy. Had I known this dream would be rattled after such an early span, I would have provided much more.

More *LOVE.*

More *JOY.*

More *HAPPINESS for life.*

Above all, I would have struggled even *HARDER* just to endure her *PAIN.*

Yet does any one of us know what we have to bear?

Love forever,

Mom

> "Man, that's the last time you'll put ya
> hands on me ..."

CHAPTER ONE

Damaged Goods

As a suburban family, we lived outside of the city of Chicago, some thirty miles south. The area wasn't big enough to be called a city, so it was known as a village. And the population was approximately 2,500. The family home measured some 980 square feet. It was a little frame house, red and white, with four small bedrooms, one bathroom, a full-sized kitchen and living room, with a big backyard. When our parents first bought that house (sometime around 1955), it wasn't equipped with a gas or electric furnace. It had one of those huge outdoor, stand-alone tanks for heating. Mom never let that tank get bone dry, though. If my memory doesn't fail me, the fuel delivery person would come every four weeks to fill it up.

"Oooh weee, it's gonna be a cold winter. Time to winterize!" Mom would tell us, dragging her words out. "Take this tape out there and wrap those pipes. Ya'll wrap 'em good and tight, y'hear? Wouldn't want 'em to freeze up on us."

Wrapping the pipes wasn't a job any of us was fond of, and yet it had to be done. It was eighteen years later when mom converted that heating unit from oil to gas, and what a big difference it made. It meant no more wrapping those pipes!

Even now, it's hard to imagine how all eight of us lived in that tiny frame house. But we did! I had five siblings: two sisters and three brothers. Dana was the eldest, and the one we looked up to for guidance and support. Lyndia, the baby sister, was a spoiled brat and a pistol at times. Johnny Jr. was the eldest son and referred to as Junior. Junior was the spitting image of Dad, and he grew up to be a lost soul. (Matter of fact, Junior and I were the only kids that resembled Dad.) Bobby, the second-eldest son, had a great creative mind. It took very little effort for him to take a gadget apart and put it back together. So when Bobby got a degree from the DeVry Institute of Technology, it was not unexpected. And Tommy, the baby brother, was the youngest of the clan.

Although we were raised with strong Christian values, our family worshipped from three different religious perspectives. Mother's missionary work was under the Pentecostal faith. Nearly every church she attended had "The Church of Jesus Christ" tagged to its name. Many times, Mom received the Holy Spirit and spoke in tongues. Dad became a member of the Methodist religion and attended the United Methodist Church down on Martin Luther King Drive in Chicago. The Second Baptist Church on 150th Street in Harvey was where one of my cousins played the organ and piano, so for my brothers and sisters, along with other relatives, this neighborhood church was the one we attended.

My mother, Esther Lee, was a retired coach cleaner for the Pennsylvania Railroad in Chicago. She was a Southern woman who spoke in a soft, passive tone. Mom was somewhat submissive in her marital relationship. Esther Lee, in her stockinged feet, stood five foot seven; her lower legs were curvy and hairy. The hair on her head was charcoal black, real wavy, thick, and hung down her back. It was always parted down the middle, combed to the back, and twisted into a bun roll. Sometimes she'd use just a little water to keep the edges slick. It was against Mom's religion to wear pants, so she wore long Christian-style dresses that hid those gorgeous legs. Even as teenagers, those churchgoing traits were instilled in us. It didn't matter how old we were—in Mom's house, everyone went to church.

"Sunday is the Lord's Day, and we must worship him. Everyone get up and get ready, now," Mom would tell us.

Every Sunday, off to church we went. At the Baptist Church, Sunday mornings were spent embracing Bible studies and morning worship services. After studying the Bible, the deacons would start with devotion as the first part of the service. The congregation would lead in by singing old gospel hymns, then praying, testifying, reading the scriptures, and taking up an offering. Once church services began around 11 a.m., there were more hymns, responsive readings, the passing of collection plates, sermons, and an altar call—but not without plenty of shouting going on. Services concluded with the pastor giving his benediction (the blessings). Staying in the church really made a difference when we were growing up. Some things we just wouldn't do because they were unrighteous. In our relationships as siblings, yeah, we fought among ourselves, but we were always mindful and respectful of others. Who on the block didn't know us Johnny-and-Esther-Lee's kids? Although Mom had old-fashioned ways in raising us, everyone knew she served the Lord. My mom was a nurturing person and gave her best to provide a safe and healthy environment. She would pray day and night.

Their marriage lacked emotional support and balance. Dad's relationship with Mom became more obsessive and abusive. His crazed behavior made our family dysfunctional. Dad might have been a decent provider for us, but he was not a good husband. A lot of times, he was full of evil; some say he was as evil as the devil.

Many times, the thoughts in my mind echoed: *How can a person keep doing the things he does and still go to church on Sundays?*

It meant nothing to Dad when he hit Mom with his belt. "You have real issues and ya need to address them," Mom would say in her soft, passive voice.

But Dad kept a solemn look on his face and never acknowledged her words. There was a very slick, sick, deep dark side to him. Keeping his demons suppressed inside had to be torture. In Dad's family, there was a pack of hidden skeletons stored away in the closet.

My dad, Johnny Sr., worked for the Pennsylvania Railroad in Chicago as a pipe fitter. And that's where he met Mom. Dad, a Southern guy, wasn't only handsome—he was a rolling stone. Tall and clean-shaven, he had a small trimmed mustache, and his hair was a mass of silky black curls. He used Murray's grease to keep the curls intact. It had one of those strong holds and gave a great shine—that pomade did the job. Dad was always dressed as sharp as a tack; he stayed in his three-piece suit even when he was hanging around the house. Now, you've heard the phrase, "Papa was a rolling stone." Yes, indeed, Dad made his rounds with the women. Don't think Mom didn't know about his flings. But despite all that messing around, my dad took care of his responsibilities; maybe that's what mattered. Well, not only that, Mom was a praying woman. But it wasn't enough, 'cause Dad wanted a separation.

One by one he called us into the den, with Mom by his side, looking grim. When it was my turn, Dad spoke in a deep harsh tone.

"Ahem. Your mother and I have some bad news to tell you kids. You know I love her, but we can't stay together. So we need to know who you'd like to live with, me or your mother."

I had always been Daddy's girl, but I sat in silence. After a minute or two, I replied, "I love you, Dad, I do, but Mom needs me. She's the one I want to live with."

"Okay, I understand. But, should you need me, I'm only a phone call away. I'll be checking on y'all regularly."

Junior was the only one who went to live with Dad. I was glad I didn't follow Dad. They moved to Chicago and stayed with a relative. But my brother spent holidays and summer vacations with us.

Guess my parents' separation wasn't a complete shock. Those two were destined to split up anyway.

There were times Dad got violent and fought with Mom. When it happened, us youngsters gathered together and wrapped around each other, each of us boo-hooing and bawling. It wasn't until we became teenagers that we four eldest banded together to stop Dad from his violent, evil ways.

I don't recall which of my siblings said, "Next time Daddy fights Mommy with the belt, let's jump him."

The rest of us replied, "Yeah, let's take him down!"

For Dad, it was a good thing it didn't happen, because the odds were against him four to one. It was during their last battle that Mom took a stand. That incident with the broom wasn't intentional. It started when Dad had hemmed Mom in the washroom. He lifted his hand and struck her.

Mom's voice crackled as she shouted, "Man, that's the last time you'll put ya hands on me. I've had it! All these years, I've been tippy-toeing and keeping the blinders on. Naw, they come off today! You bring those women into our home and have intimate relationships with 'em! Then when I walk in on ya, you shout out for me to get out of the room? Ya strike out and fight when the mood hits ya. The things you've done to this family. It's a wonder the kids ain't affected. Man, may God have mercy on your soul!"

After lashing out, Mom turned and grabbed a broom that stood against the furnace door. But as she raised it over her head, the broom handle hit the ceiling light. The glass broke and shattered into tiny pieces all over Dad. He jumped back and yelled in his deep, harsh tone, "Woman, what type of God do you serve?"

Of course, Dad refused to go to the hospital. So, they spent the next hours plucking tiny glass particles from his dark, bruised skin. And it was the God who Mother served that put some fear in him. Dad never again struck Mom. My siblings may not recall the details of what was said, nor the incident. But this whole scene and my parents' words stuck with me through the years. After witnessing the evil things done, my thoughts rang: *Dad's an example of damaged goods.*

Our punishments were nothing like what he put Mom through. Whenever one of us was to be disciplined, he told us, "Go ahead and hold that hand out."

Then he slowly took off his thick, black leather belt and whacked it in the palm of our hand—about ten times. That was the extent of his discipline for us. I don't recall everything I'd done to get punished. But there was one incident when he woke me up for not doing the dishes before going to bed. You can bet I never did that again. Every time he'd whack me, I'd tighten up my body, scrunch up my face, and hold out a firm palm—with all five fingers spread apart. I took those licks and stood there, rolling my eyes at him with each stroke and wanting to ask, "Are you tired now, 'cause that doesn't even hurt." I'd only thought it; I never said it. I wouldn't dare back-talk Dad and push his buttons. Plus, I wasn't that tough as a kid or adolescent. It was rare to be disciplined by him, anyway. Dad never physically abused any of his kids; Mom was the one he sought. He didn't show an ounce of kindness when it came to her. Dad had real issues; he was toxic and poisonous. Think about it: What kinda man whips his wife with a belt? Isn't that a sign of a deeply troubled man?

The memory gets kind of fuzzy. I don't recall all the details, just the gist of the story. And this one added another blemish to darken Dad's character.

It happened the time Bobby took the Halsted Street bus to Chicago, where he met Dad for lunch. When Bobby arrived at the restaurant on 73rd Street, Dad was already seated, sipping black coffee. Dad loved coffee without any cream or sugar, and would always order a delicious pecan roll. While they sat there talking, the waitress returned to refill Dad's coffee cup and take Bobby's order.

In his deep tone, Dad introduced the waitress to Bobby. Turning to face the waitress, he told her, "This is my nephew."

"It totally threw me for a loop when Dad made that statement," Bobby told me. "Dad didn't have the decency to let the waitress know I was his son. He called me his nephew. Sis, I was so speechless and hurt that I just didn't say anything to him."

When my brother shared this experience, I too felt the pain. Although I was Daddy's girl, some things just can't be excused. When Dad split from the family, we four eldest had grown and were nearing adulthood. Lyndia and Tommy were still tots.

Now, there won't be any more time spent rehashing my siblings' adventures growing up. They're not the real focus of the story. So, those childhood memories shall remain in the past.

The Insight

A ton of thoughts swirled around my head. *Was Dad abused as a kid to be such a toxic person? What pleasure had he gotten treating a good woman like that? Did his actions go back to before any of us were born? Did he act like that while they dated? Had Mom just chosen the wrong person to marry? Why did Mom stay so long in a toxic relationship? The things that went on in our house could've easily damaged any one sibling. Did it?*

"Yep, I'm married, but we don't live
together. . . ."

CHAPTER TWO

Broken Vows

After watching Mom and Dad, having a husband wasn't something I wanted. Basically I thought, "I'll never stay with any man who wants to hurt me."

Growing up in a toxic environment made a deep imprint on my heart. I was the second-eldest child, Daddy's girl. People would tell me, "You're the striking image of your dad. You even got a lot of his traits. But wait, I see those delicate features of your mama in you."

It appeared I had inherited a little of this and a little of that from both parents. When it came to height, I was a little shorty and somewhere around five foot five. I had a keen, oval-shaped face with a nice dark chocolate complexion, big brown eyes accented with thick black eyebrows, long lashes, a small nose, luscious thin lips, and a full head of long, black, curly and wavy hair. I always wore my hair parted down the middle and pulled back into a braided ponytail with a ribbon at the end.

With both parents, I had close-knit relationships and embraced each in their own special way. Although Mom never spoke about the birds and bees, her spiritual views kept me grounded, scholarly, and astute. I looked up to her as the kind, gentle, and nurturing parent she was. And I did whatever it took not to cause her grief. She was easy to talk to and always encouraging.

Whenever she told me, "I believe in you," it would stroke my ego.

As for Dad, he wreaked havoc in the family. But it was his nurturing and love that made me feel warm and secure. At an early age, I found pleasure in pleasing him. He always made sure I got everything my heart desired, and it meant so much. Many times he said, "I love you unconditionally. You are the apple of my eye."

Of course I felt special. I must admit those words brought me joy and made me want to shine. I tried to be the best at school and not chase after boys. I would tell him how good he was, respect his opinion, and always find something comforting to say.

Being perfect helps me dodge the line of fire, I thought.

One of the ways I escaped my family's friction was through my invisible-self mode. I could fade within myself—but still be aware of my surroundings. I would relax my mind, stand completely still, close my eyes, and imagine what it felt like to be invisible. I would continuously repeat the words: "I'm invisible. I'm invisible. I'm invisible. I'm invisible."

When I wasn't in that particular mindset, I'd think of careers I wanted to have after graduation. *How about having a career that takes you places, paying big bucks?* I thought to myself. *Why not an airline flight attendant? How about signing up for the Armed Forces and working to get a high rank? What about being a model? How about being an actress?*

There were all types of beautiful careers inside my wandering mind. Never lacking self-confidence, I knew my dreams were possible. Despite my naïveté and vulnerability, I've always been a dreamer about one thing or another.

The time I thought about becoming a preacher, I told my folks, "When I become an adult, I'm gonna be a preacher and make all the money. I'm going to talk the talk so I can walk the walk."

In his deep voice, Dad responded, "I can see that. You always have a good sermon to tell us at the dinner table. So how about I start calling you Preacher?"

In a zestful tone, I agreed. "Yeah, Dad, that's right! Call me Preacher from now on!"

From then on, even when my uncles came by for their music rehearsals, they'd call out, "Come on Preacher, lead us in a prayer before we start practicing!"

So that's how I inherited the nickname Preacher. After releasing a powerful prayer, I hung around just to hear those brothers harmonize. As a renowned group, they were best known for their vocals in the gospel industry. For years they performed in gospel venues alongside the likes of the Staple Singers and Willie Dixon, among others. And their musical talent was embraced by many gospel lovers.

Well, I didn't mind doing my fair share at home, either. I'd pitch in with watching my siblings and doing all the housework. My siblings would say, "Sis, can't nobody clean a house like you. You'd make a good maid."

When it came time to clean, I'd get on my siblings and tell them, "Y'all better move your stuff out of this living room or lose it. 'Cause I'm about to throw it in the garbage."

Since I'd done this before, they knew not to test me. I was a great little cleaner, and I would work my tail off. As for the cooking, Dana took the lead on that, being the eldest.

But when I wasn't home, they'd find me hanging out over at Netti's house. Netti was a close friend and lived around the corner in an apartment complex. We'd been friends since the age of nine. We both attended the same schools, from grammar through to our senior year. I was known in their family as "Netti's little buddy."

During the summer break, we'd separate. Usually, I'd visit family in Chicago, but one summer, I wasn't going. I'd planned to hang out with my best friend Netti. When we returned to school, I'd start my senior year.

Forget going to Chicago. Netti's brother Craig is coming from the Navy, I reminded myself.

Craig was a cool person, but a little egotistical. Guess he thought he was all that and a bag of chips. In my eyes, he was. Craig always walked with a good posture and stared a person dead in the eyes when they talked. He stood five foot ten, with a dark-toned complexion, deep brown, beady eyes, a short pudgy nose, and a stocky build. He had no eyebrows, which did look rather strange. But his smooth talk made up for that flaw. Boy, he reminded me so much of Dad. They both were sharp dressers, quick thinkers, smooth talkers, and definitely ladies' men. Craig even blew those perfect smoke rings that floated in the air as he exhaled his cigarette smoke, the same way Dad would've done it.

When Craig pulled up in his flashy white Thunderbird convertible, I hadn't seen him since I was around twelve. And that had been five or six years ago. Now he'd no longer think of me as Netti's little buddy, but as a woman. I gazed into his brown eyes, bucked wide open. His look gave the impression that he found me appealing. This was going to be the beginning of a great summer!

As we stood face-to-face, Craig grinned and asked, "So, you're Netti's little buddy, huh? I see you're not little no more. How about I take you on a date?"

With a bashful smile, I replied, "Yeah, I'd go out with you."

Since I had never been on a date, I thought, *What should I wear? How should I act? How would he act?*

I decided to wear my tight, low-cut red and black mini dress with black fishnet stockings and red and black pumps. This look showed every curve on my tiny physique, enough to catch any man's eye. When I opened the door, his beady little eyes scanned my body. I had grown into a full woman, and it showed. *But had I truly reached womanhood? Although it felt real, was it?* These questions are what I'd asked myself. Here is where the story should've ended. But in reality, that's where it all began.

That night, Craig and I hung out with his best friend, Eddie, and his girlfriend, Barbara. Eddie was also one of those smooth-talking dudes. He loved to wear those big, wide-brimmed hats, tilted to one side. And this cat strutted like a pimp. On the other hand, Barbara appeared to be very mild and humble, even passive. They were such a mismatched couple. For the four of us, it wasn't easy deciding on what to do. But we drove to the lakefront and stayed to watch the sunrise. While there, we watched the sun come up and listened to those old war stories. Don't quite recall heads or tails of what was spoken about those war days, but my eyebrows rose a notch when I discovered that Barbara and Craig's wife, Renna, were best of friends. They were thicker than thieves.

Who could've imagined such a thing? Craig was a married man! Aha, married and out on a date—how bold was he? Netti and I were supposed to be the best of friends, yet she never spoke about her brother being married.

Riding home in the back seat of Craig's car, his hand gently touched my thigh as he whispered sweet nothings in my ear. But he didn't realize this conversation wasn't appropriate. I was pure as the virgin oil. We talked about purification for the next few minutes. Uh-huh, how dare Craig bring Eddie and Barbara in on our conversation, only to laugh at me! As soon as Craig saw the anger upon my face—my scrunched up eyelids, gritted teeth, clenched jaw, and a horrible frown—there was nothing but silence. When it broke, I began to find out more about the man I was with. In his mind, he believed his marriage wasn't truly a marriage.

"Yep, I'm married, but we don't live together. I've not seen or been with her since being home from the Navy. See, it's just like not being married," he said.

> Stepping back to reflect on a moment of epiphany.
>
> Yes, I was young, vulnerable, and extremely naïve to have indulged in such an illicit affair. And if there's blame to be shouldered, it's shared between the two of us—me for being vulnerable and naïve, and him for his dishonesty and those broken vows. Most importantly, he was older and should have known better. We'd committed a sinful act, not only against ourselves, but against another as well.
>
> Often, a person releases one guilt only to harbor another. Ending our relationship would have been the righteous and healthiest thing to have done, since marriage vows mustn't be taken lightly. This was truly a lesson I've learned.

During those summer days, we continued to see each other—but neither Netti nor our parents had an inkling about the relationship. Many times he said, "I'm your man, and you're my woman."

Seems men do all they can to emotionally control your being. Shucks, the way Daddy acted in our home really twisted my mind. Craig had messed with my head, too, feeding me his lines.

His charm fed on the vulnerability of my existence. I just didn't have the nerve to tell Mom and Dad about this guy. That was because they thought of me as a good girl. I'd found myself rationalizing why we should have a relationship. Yeah, I had known he was married, but he'd said he was separated . . . plus, he'd made my heart flutter. We'd meshed in so many ways. It's all good; nothing wrong with just talking. I had enjoyed our conversations and being in his company. Those darn butterflies churning my stomach—like a booming presence. That was what kept me hanging in there; my stomach had been booming from way back. It wasn't just the way he'd blown those smoke rings, like Dad had done, or the flattering lines he fed me.

Craig had the kind of personality that ignited those fireflies a long time ago. He was always attired in black, styling and profiling from head to toe. He stepped with confidence and swag, his posture straight and tall. He was gifted with those finely tuned abs and biceps. Craig had a chilled-out body language that oozed calmness and a can-do, I'm-the-man attitude. He kept abreast of worldly issues—could hold onto any topic. His smarts were stimulated when he was tucked away behind a book, newspaper, or something of interest. He was always exercising his brain. And there was nothing like his scent, so aromatic, especially accented with a whiff of his manly-smelling cologne.

His affectionate ways had taken me to another high. The warmth of his face brushed against mine.

His tongue swirled wet kisses around my neck. And the tantalizing touches of his manly hand on my inner thigh as he lightly caressed me with his fingertips . . . Those times he'd wink, as if offering a flirty word or two. He'd turn the corner of his lip and flash that sexy, wicked, sweet smile— which would make those butterflies flutter.

The day arrived when Craig convinced me to take our relationship to another stage—from teen to womanhood. Craig knew he was the man to capture my heart. He was the first man I'd ever been with. I'd fallen for him quickly, hard, and fast. Then again, love is blind. I'd put him on a pedestal that would undoubtedly tumble over.

It was the year 1970 when my dad became deathly ill. He was only 47 years old and suffered from three serious health problems: severe pulmonary edema, congestive bronchopneumonia, and coronary artery disease. It was at the VA Hospital in Hines, Illinois, that Dad called us to his bedside. We all stared at the tracheal tube that stuck out from his neck.

Dad no longer talked in his harsh tone. He spoke in a slow, soft, whispery voice, and said, "Kids, come close. I want to tell you something, pay attention now. Listen to your mother. I'm sorry for the way I treated her. I apologize and love you all."

He not only wanted to be forgiven by his kids, but told Mom, "Please forgive me for all the wrong I've done you. I do love you."

In spite of everything he had put her through, Mom said, "I forgive you. And I love you, too." Perhaps she forgave him because she was a Christian woman.

Dad loved his unfiltered Pall Mall cigarettes; he smoked them for years. Soon as he put out one cig, he'd light another. He'd smoke until the burning ash touched his fingertips. The entire ashtray would be filled with those smelly cigarette butts as the smoky odor filtered through the house. Today we'd call his toxic habit being a chain-smoker. It's a title that can lead to death.

The news about Dad's illness wasn't the worst. There was something more mystifying! I'd begun working during the summer and wasn't feeling well. So, I went to see the doctor. He ran a few tests and told me the results would come later. When the phone rang, I thought, *Could this mean I'm going to be a mom?*

The mere fact of telling Dad wasn't happening. Growing up with parents with traditional principles, how could I explain coming into motherhood without being married? At 10 p.m. on July 23, 1970, we got the news that Dad had made his transition. Although I still had one parent, I couldn't forget Dad and the close relationship we shared. Dad was gone. He was gone forever and wasn't coming back. I cried so hard. I isolated myself from my family. Learning of his death was emotionally challenging—as if life had robbed me. Something inside me was broken. My emotions were exploding all over the place. I felt unprotected, angered, lost, totally abandoned, and relieved. He'd given me so much and would've done anything for me. I'd always miss hearing him say, "I love you unconditionally."

He loved me, yet he left me. It was the first time someone I bonded with and loved had died. Sure, Dad had his way of acting out, but that had never taken away my love for him. On the other hand, I felt a sense of relief knowing Dad would discover his true inner being in another place and time. God had given Mom back her life to find peace and healing from her wounds. Dad's demise left me with many damaging scars to carry in life. It has been said that in a family, when one leaves this earth, another life is born. And so it was—I was pregnant.

Mom took the news calmly when I blurted out, "Guess what, you're going to be a grandma! I'm around six weeks along. It's not one of my dreams either: it's real."

She asked, "Are you getting married?"

I replied, "No, Mom, he's married already. But I'm gonna have my baby anyway and give it lots of love. The way Dad acted . . . I don't want a husband. Maybe one day I'll get married for my baby's sake. Every child needs a dad. I'm going to stay here till I find us a place."

With a smile on her face, she said, "So—I'm really going to be a grandma, huh?"

───◆───

The next day, I didn't hesitate. "Craig, guess what? I took that rabbit test, and the rabbit died."

Shocked and silent, he shook his head back and forth and said, "You can't be! It only happened that one time."

I replied, "Uh-huh, once was all it took."

His face wrinkled with anger. "We don't need to be in this relationship. I'm married and already have a kid. I can't do this anymore."

Craig continued whining about how he wanted out of the relationship—grasping hold of his marriage vows. It was the typical response of a man busted with his pants down. What's done in the dark surely comes to light. The time to turn back had long past—but did he care?

After two months, I found out Craig's wife was approaching motherhood as well. Only difference was that she was due in January, and I'd follow in March. This would be Craig's second child with Renna.

There was very little I knew about Renna. She was his wife and the mother of his children, and I was entangled in their marriage. It was a guilt I bore deep inside. Craig once said, "She's full of anger and can carry a mean streak. Sometimes she's as fiery as her red hair."

I remembered the sole picture I'd seen at Netti's house, on their small round end table. I'd thought it was a family member—appears it was Renna, with her thin, pale face and flaming red hair.

During my pregnancy, I had continuously phoned and attempted to visit Netti. But she wouldn't return my calls and was never at home. It was apparent she no longer wanted to embrace our relationship. Was it because I was carrying her brother's baby and she'd chosen to distance herself? I had surmised that was the case. As puzzling as it was, I never discovered the true reason.

But her rejection had thrown me onto a seesaw of emotions. I went from crying and sobbing to freaking out over the smallest things. I had a really hard time coping. This went on for several weeks of the pregnancy. But as the loss of our friendship faded, I came to the realization that if she ever came back, there'd be no questions asked. It was weird not having Netti around, but I had to push through and move forward.

I wouldn't graduate senior year with the rest of the class. When school started back in August, I had to transfer to a program for unwed moms. We were a sight to see, all of us teenage moms waddling around with our big bellies. Since we'd only go three days a week, it wasn't bad. Being pregnant and having a life growing inside was a wonderful, challenging experience. On the road to mommyhood, I'd gained a feeling of freshness as my body went through the hormonal changes. I'd put on plenty of weight—from 105, I packed on around 45 more pounds.

Every now and then, my back ached something awful. And going from an A to a C cup, my breasts had gotten more sensitive, especially around the nipples. Although my breasts didn't hurt, they just felt kind of jiggly, like there was liquid inside 'em. I felt a stretching sensation around my abdomen, and at times there was a twitch of pain. I had even swollen up round the ankles and fingers; my face was bloated like a basketball. One good thing was that I hadn't experienced morning sickness like some of the others, whose unsettled stomachs kept them from coming to class.

Inside, I hurt so badly not having Craig around. It was as if my heart had been ripped out. I had given myself to him, and even though he knew about my pregnancy, he wanted no part. That's what hurt even more. And to think, I loved him unconditionally. Words could not describe the depth of my emotion. I cried until my teardrops dried up. Being pregnant and alone was a hard and painful journey. I started journaling to lighten my pain.

With Netti and I no longer close, my friend Peaches often visited. Peaches came to our small suburban town from Joliet to enter her freshman year in high school. Fortunately, she lived in the district where I attended Thornton Township High School. Right away, we established a relationship, calling ourselves "home girls." Peaches stood five foot eight with a medium complexion, round face, and beautifully slanted eyes. She was a curvy, full-figured woman with full hips paired with an even larger bust. She wore her hair cut short and tapered in the back.

The fact that I was going to be somebody's mommy brought a cluster of mixed emotions. At times I was happy. Sometimes I was sad. And at other moments, I felt nervous and daunted. I was so happy to be having my own bundle of joy, yet sad that I wouldn't have a partner to share in the parenting. My nerves got jittery worrying about the financial aspect. The whole idea of parenting was very frightening.

"Peaches, I don't think I can do this parent thing," I told her, bursting into tears.

Whenever I made that statement, she'd comment, "You're just feeling overwhelmed again, naturally. You are going to be a *terrific* mom."

Throughout my pregnancy, I was lucky to have Peaches taking on a supportive and nurturing role. Thinking about Craig with his wife during her pregnancy only hurt me. But realistically, I wasn't alone. Mom and Peaches stood alongside me for comfort and support. My life was headed to a turning point—soon I'd be some little baby's mommy.

"Looks like you're carrying that baby mighty high. It's a girl," Mom said with a grin.

"Is that right? Well, I best get started picking names, huh?" I told her as we chuckled. I threw out some names: "LaToya, LaTanya, LaShawna, Jade, Queen, Princess, Precious, and Treasure. Oh yeah, and there's China. How's that for starters?" I said, smiling.

By year-end, Peaches and my sister Dana had gotten jobs with the same company. They felt I should apply, too. Since my delivery date wasn't for three months, I could have a job waiting afterward. Once I returned the application, I was put on the waiting list to take a federal test. Eventually I was called to come down and take the exam. I passed with flying colors and scored a 99 percent. When the first letter arrived, reality set in. I realized that I was in my seventh month of pregnancy, with a job offer.

Who'd want to hire me like this? I asked myself.

I wasn't ready to face working life. So when that second letter came, I called the number.

"Sorry, I can't take the job right now. Best you don't call me—I'll call you," I told the person who answered.

Actually, the only offer I wanted was for Craig to step up and own up to his responsibilities. This journey has ended; Craig's shoe prints will go in one direction and mine another.

The Insight

As I think back and analyze some things, it's pretty clear that I inherited a little of Mom's behavioral traits as well, and this one was a biggie: picking the wrong person and expecting the best. When it came to men, the ones we both picked were toxic. Then again, something in me must have adored toxicity; Dad was full of poison, and some rubbed off on me. I was cursed from the start! Guess I was born with a little of both these worldly traits within me.

CHAPTER THREE

The Birth

China was born on March 24, 1971, at Ingalls Hospital in Harvey, Illinois. She weighed ten pounds and fifteen ounces. Gosh, that was a pretty big baby to have come through my birth canal! Surprisingly, they didn't try to induce my labor or attempt a C-section. The pain felt like my skin was being turned inside out. After the delivery, I stared down at her baby face. Cuddling her in my arms, I saw she had a nose like Craig's—a pudgy one. I hadn't seen him during the entire nine months, yet he showed up at the hospital.

At first we just stared at each other. Then I asked, "Why are you here?"

He responded, "Oh, I came to see the baby. It's a girl, huh?"

"Yeah, and she looks just like you," I replied. It was apparent he didn't want to hear that.

As he slowly backed out of the room, he asked, "Tell me the truth, you sure she's mine?"

"Yup, and it can be proven," I said. "I'm going to prove it to you."

"Well, whatever works for you. I can't be a father to her. You chose to keep the baby, so that's the choice you've made."

Again, he tried to worm his way out of our lives. But this time, the ball would be in my court. Once the DNA test was taken, the results showed he had planted the seed. And that was something he couldn't wriggle out of!

After I gave birth, my life changed rapidly and drastically. The thoughts going through my mind were kicking my butt. I could hear the words loud and clear: *You're guilty as sin.*

Coming from a Christian upbringing, I was consumed with all kinds of guilt. Yes, indeed, I'd shamed the family by having a relationship with a married man and giving birth out of wedlock. Back in those days, this type of toxic behavior was downright unrighteous and sinful.

I'd never done the mommy scene before. But there I was, a single parent. Being a mom—and the custodial parent—was a huge challenge. I'd have to be both mother and father, which meant I'd have to juggle my responsibilities, my finances, and my time. Down the road, the greatest task of all would be explaining to China why she didn't have a dad in her life. But for now, it was about building the parent-child relationship, nurturing her needs, establishing a routine, ensuring stability and child care, finishing school, going to work, making ends meet, and spending quality time together. I was faced with two important jobs: being a parent and earning a living. And that was a heck of a responsibility to have to go alone.

Besides the guilt, my emotions were all mixed into one big blob, with one clear feeling for sure: I felt so darn scared going it alone. Wow! Taking care of my baby wasn't going to be easy, but she'd have me to raise her. Frankly, that wasn't enough; I wanted her to have a dad in her life. As you know, my dad was a toxic one. In response to Craig's negative attitude, my toxic traits wanted to lash out, just as Dad would've. But I kept it all contained, knowing what a wonderful opportunity he was missing by not being a part of her life. All I could give was an abundance of love for the two of us, which meant loving her with every fiber of my being. Despite those toxic emotions, I loved the baby I brought into this world. I couldn't take back our affair. At that time, I didn't care what anyone thought—Mom, Dad, my sisters, brothers, relatives, or friends. I was young and naïve, and I deeply loved Craig.

It came out of nowhere, that incredible fear. The fear of the unknown, and that I had to go it alone. So, I wasn't as brave and fearless as I'd thought. But I was brazen enough to take on a journey looking for Mr. Right, that special someone who could be a dad to my baby. Any man can be a father, but it takes a real man to be a dad.

You need a man to be complete. It'll make us whole, I thought.

A man could nurture and love us, protect and provide for us. This was all ingrained in my feminine psyche. I knew my path would cross with a few men, if only to build a foundation. Whether these relationships turned out to be good or bad, I felt incomplete and would go on an insatiable hunt. Above all, I was determined to give my baby what she deserved in life. For me, that meant the love of two parents and everything that came with that.

I returned to school to finish my education. It was the chance I needed to start a better life as a single parent. Although I wouldn't graduate with my classmates, at least I'd have a diploma. After Dad's death, Mom's income barely took care of our food and clothing.

After dating for a year, Dana and Larry finally got married. She'd given birth to a set of twins, a girl and boy. But her baby boy only lived three days and died at the Little Company of Mary Hospital. Hearing that news, I felt numb. Dana had had a little baby I'd never meet, and I felt her pain. As the tears rolled down my cheeks, I felt so empty inside. I wasn't sure if the emptiness was for my sister and her loss, or for not being able to know her little angel. The one thing I knew was that I had to be there whenever she was ready to talk. In the face of her loss, it wasn't about giving advice, but listening and sharing time with her. I could only hope my presence would make a difference. As time passed, she never spoke about it. And I had to respect her choice—those were her memories.

Now that I was a parent, I needed to contribute more, so I'd gotten a job working in Chicago at Evans down on State Street. Back then, the retail stores only paid $1.60 an hour. I was told that public aid would subsidize my income and go after Craig for support. That was my chance for a new start. So, off we went to live in the big city of Chicago. I'd found a cozy studio apartment on the southeast side of town. I can still recall the address: 1972 East 73rd Place. It was so convenient, with public transportation stopping right in front of our apartment and the little shopping mall on 71st and Jeffery within walking distance. It was a great area to live in, especially for a first apartment.

Once I started dating, I met this fellow, Marcus Whiting. Marcus was clean-shaven and stood five foot six, weighed around 175 pounds, and kept his hair in a short fade. He was a groovy kinda guy and the lead singer of a rock group. His band played regularly at the Pumpkin Room, a lounge on the corner of 71st and Jeffery. Back then, this was the hangout where all the happenings were. He'd always come onstage wearing his black, gold, and red scarf wrapped around his head in a bandana style. Whenever Marcus sang, he swayed seductively. His performances were out of this world, which was what attracted me to him. Even when I heard they were playing out of state, I was right there to listen to the band. Mom would babysit, and I had my little red 1972 Nova to get around in.

There was one time I asked Peaches, "Want to take a road trip to Saginaw, Michigan? It's only 450 miles, and we can pull an all-nighter."

Peaches eagerly replied, "Why not? That sounds like fun."

When we arrived, our faces were already familiar. Some of the band members called us "groupies."

When the band took a break, Marcus approached us and asked, "Can I buy you two a drink? How about you lovely ladies meet us backstage?"

"We'll think about that." I blushed, looking down to hide my cheeks.

All the time we talked, I felt a warm rush passing through my body. Backstage we even hung out with the Emotions (Jeanette, Wanda, and Sheila—or was it Pamela?). I'm sure you recall this group. Their hit singles were "So I Can Love You," "The Best of a Love Affair," "Heart Association," "I've Fallen In Love," "Show Me How," "I Wanna Come Back," "What Do the Lonely Do at Christmas," and many other great tunes. We had a bang-up time watching those performers. And it was obvious we'd taken a liking to being on their scene. They just couldn't figure out which of us was fishing. That was great, 'cause Marcus was doing some baiting and I wanted to be his catch. My heart started pounding knowing he was on the prowl. Rumor had it that Marcus had gone with a real foxy chick. She was the lead singer in one of those popular R&B groups. That didn't faze me; why wouldn't they be coupled? They traveled in the same circles, and I'd just come on the scene.

Our first date was a dinner at one of those Hyde Park restaurants.

"So, tell me something about yourself," he said, as the candlelight gleamed.As our eyes locked, I said softly, "I just love rock music. I'm a working single mom. I'm raising a baby girl who I adore. She's only a few months old. And we get in our mommy-time together. On my days off, we take a stroll around Lincoln Park or Brookfield Zoo, the Museum of Science and Industry, Fun Town, or the shopping malls. Oh yeah, we'll even have our baby picnic outings at times. We live in a studio apartment on the South Side. And there's no man in our life. Are you single? Do you have kids?" I asked.

Marcus replied, "Yes, I'm single, and no—no kids."

"Well, do you even like 'em?" I asked, concerned.

"Yeees," he answered, dragging out the word.

"That's good, because the person who loves me needs to love my baby," I replied openly.

"I'm diggin' you on that," he smirked.

After that night, we continued to see each other. When he wasn't doing a gig, he'd come by the house for dinner. Sometimes we'd just have a pizza with a side of vegetables.

One time, Marcus said, "Having dinner here gives me a chance to spend time with your baby. I want her to see me around you. Already I can tell she seems to like it when I'm around."

Even as a baby, China kept a little smile on her face as Marcus picked her up to play. Our relationship blossomed. Out of the blue, Marcus surprised me when he came to Evans to have lunch with me. That was something he'd never done before—coming down to have lunch.

As we sat side by side at the cafeteria table, he said, "I realize how much I love you. I want to marry you and be there for your baby. I don't have a ring, but that comes later. What do you say to that, baby?"

As my heart raced, I sat in silence, thinking, *Could this be? Have I found someone who wants us on the first go around? Is this relationship a dream? Did he just ask to marry us? Is he really good marriage material?*

After the thoughts cleared, I reached for his hand and said, "I love you, too, baby. Yes, I'll be your wife, and you'll be a dad to my baby. We'll start making plans after I get that ring."

That night, I was so elated about his proposal. I told China, "Mommy is going to get married and you'll have a daddy soon. How'd you like that?"

It's a good thing to talk with your baby through all their developmental stages. Their little eyes light up when you speak to them. When she responded with that goo-goo ga-ga talk, I took it that she agreed. Babies can be smart, you know. Looking back, perhaps she was warning me about him. That's something I should have considered.

Marcus was living with his sister even though they bumped heads every now and then. Although we'd planned to marry, he'd go back and forth from his place to mine. Hanging out with Marcus wasn't easy. Sometimes he'd do a switcheroo—Dr. Jekyll and Mr. Hyde. Whenever Peaches and her husband Linc came by, Marcus would become very combative with Linc, and possessive of me. Marcus would go into a rage, wanting to attack Linc's every phrase. Can't quite remember his exact words, but it was obvious that there was no type of relationship between them.

Linc was tall, with beautiful dark skin, a mustache, and a muscular build; he was very handsome. You see, Linc was his rival. He too played in a rock group. Matter of fact, he was a drummer and often did some lead singing. Back in the day, his group played onstage alongside the band Rufus, who sang with the Queen of Funk, Chaka Khan. That's the scene he was into! Linc was just as funky as Marcus.

I wondered if Marcus and I actually had any real romantic moments, or if it was just another rebound relationship. In the beginning, everything was smooth sailing. We couldn't get enough of one another. But life has its way of changing things as you go down the path. With the weird things Marcus was doing, I started wondering if he was into drugs. His moods were pretty wild. He'd pace the floor back and forth. Many times he talked about putting voodoo spells on people. My life with him had become a total nightmare.

He'd say, "Look at us. We are so good for each other, baby."

Then he'd trip and make jabbing comments about how I dressed. When Marcus showed his devilish side, I knew this wasn't going to be a lasting relationship.

One scene lingers in my mind. One morning, I wore my sexy black and red mini dress. And I thought I looked rather charming. Marcus did a double take, his face wrinkled with jealousy.

He said, "Don't think you're going out wearing that slutty outfit."

Before I realized it, he'd reached his hand out, grabbed the collar of my dress, and tore it. I looked down and saw the material bunched in his hand. Marcus didn't realize how lucky he was after doing something like that. As I grabbed hold of his hand before he drew it back, that ugly Dad side of me was screaming to erupt. I gritted my teeth and wanted to rip his arm right from its socket. It took a lot to control my attack mode, but I wasn't going to raise China in such an unhealthy environment. I asked myself, *What the heck? Why are you girls even with this psycho dude, anyway? It's time to get out—naw, RUN—from this madness.*

After what Marcus had done, I knew I had to follow my thoughts. I wasn't going to allow any man to think he could put his hands on me, like Mother had allowed. That was something I'd promised myself as a kid—never let a man get the best of you. Yeah, I really loved Marcus once, but his actions negated all that love. And it helped me to realize he wasn't the dad I needed for China. Nor was he the man I wanted to call my husband.

Marcus toned down his crazy behavior, became mellower, talked calmer, and was more affectionate. Even though his personality changed, our relationship had already gone sour and toxic.

He was constantly telling me, "Baby, I really adore ya'll so much."

But by then, our feelings weren't mutual. I'd seen his deepest and darkest side, and it wasn't pretty. Perhaps he'd grown to sense the relationship was one-sided. I'd become unaffectionate and distant by doing more mommy activities with China. China and I even spent time hanging out with Dana and her kids. I loved China too much and knew that Marcus wasn't a good fit for us after all.

In situations like these, we women need to ease out tactfully. A safer, more peaceful way to part—let them dump you rather than you dump them. When Marcus's ego took center stage, it panned out. No way was he gonna give 80 percent and accept a mere 20.

On the way out, he told me, "I'm a musician, baby. Women will flock to me."

I pretended to be heartbroken when he said, "Hey babe, hey—I'm out of here!"

Basically, that was his line. And he went into the night—parting can be such sweet sorrow. Although our relationship ended, I couldn't give up trying to make a life, a home, a family. This would be another shoe print on our path.

The Insight

These are the danger signs of a toxic partner and an unhealthy relationship:

• Mood swings.
• Different personalities.
• Possessiveness.
• Constant verbal or physical abuse.
• Unexpected rage for no reason.
• Need for complete control.

With Craig and I both working, we'd
decided to send China to . . .

CHAPTER FOUR

A Killer in Our Midst

W ith Marcus and I no longer a couple, I finally got a chance to interact with my neighbor, Mandy. She'd been living there all the time. Her apartment was adjacent to mine, although we never had the pleasure of socializing. Mandy was dark-skinned, short, and plump and had long, thick, wavy, jet-black hair. She was a very attractive woman. Mandy didn't work, but received public assistance. She was separated from her husband Baylee and had two beautiful daughters, Fern and Cindy. Fern was already seven, and Cindy was four years old. It took very little time for Mandy and I to bond.

When she first spoke about her husband, she said, "Baylee was a pure jerk, and I had to leave him. He liked fighting about any little thing. My house is more peaceful not having to fight. I'm going with Joey even though he is married. We've been together three years now."

By now I'd gotten another job—working at the University of Chicago Hospital in Hyde Park, where I'd assign nurses from a schedule, among other duties. The hospital was right in our neighborhood. Sometimes I'd wind up walking to work. Since I knew Mandy could use some extra cash, she'd babysit China. She taught her how to walk, talk, and potty-trained her—all before she was nine months old. We formed a close relationship. In the long run, we became the best of friends. She was my BFF.

Perhaps it was because Mandy dated a married man, like I had. Then again, I actually hadn't figured out how we took a liking to each other from the start. I just knew that we must embrace whoever comes into our lives. God placed that person there for a particular reason.

Those early days with China flew past, and I just adored her. We took trips to zoos, museums, and amusement parks when she no longer needed to be pushed in a stroller. She turned out to be a great walker and wanted to explore everything. China kept me on the go during my weekends off. The time we spent together helped me realize how precious children are, how quickly they blossom before our eyes. Even though I hadn't lived a totally Christian lifestyle, I never forgot how to pray. Every day, I'd send a prayer out to our Father above.

It went something like this: "I'm a single mom trying to make it on my own, and thank you Lord for sending me my baby. She's the sunshine of my life. I love her with all my heart and soul. I worship Your being and praise Your holy name. It is through Your glory all things are possible." Perhaps it was that prayer that got us through each day.

Then one day, he came driving down Jeffery Street in his shiny black convertible, slick as ever. Yep, it was my baby's daddy, Craig, back on the scene. When he saw me standing on the corner, he pulled to the curb and got out of the car. He was dressed in all black, looking suave from head to toe. I'd never imagined our paths would cross again, but they did!

Since China wasn't with me, he asked, "Where is my daughter? Are you going to let me see her?"

We both went into the apartment and stood in my small, narrow kitchen. My eyes connected with his, and I looked down at China and turned back to stare at Craig.

"Yeah, I do see a slight family resemblance myself," he finally said.

As he leaned over to take China in his arms, he told her, "Hi, I'm your dad."

I interjected and said, "That's your father."

Craig just chuckled as he continued to hold her. While China sat on his lap, Craig poured on his slick talk.

He turned to me and said, "Baby, how you've been doing? You know, you broke my heart when you moved away. Do you know how much I've missed you guys?"

I wasn't about to respond to his questions. I knew Craig was still the same old dude. His rap was full of crap.

He continued, "My marriage is over, I want you to know. . . . Are you seeing anyone?"

That was one question I did respond to. I replied, "Naw, I'm not seeing anyone. But we do have a daughter that I spend my time with."

Once he'd told me his marriage was over and knew I wasn't seeing anyone, Craig started trying to hitch back up. After all, he was the baby's daddy and had the right to be part of her life. But why did I allow him back in mine? That's the million-dollar question. Believe it or not, I don't know the answer. Perhaps I could have characterized myself as an idiot, stupid, desperate for love, or a love addict. But it happened, and there are no solid answers. Really, who knows why we cling to toxic relationships? There are things in life we all regret; mine just happened to be toxicity. Then again, I was one unlucky woman when it came to finding love.

Before you read on or judge, stop and think about your most regrettable moment in life.

Now, ask yourself, "Why did I do that?" You probably don't even have an answer.

It's true my life was satisfying at that time, and it seemed like nothing could have changed that. Well, something did! On my way home from the hairdresser, my foot twisted in a pothole, causing a torn ligament. On crutches for the next four weeks, I couldn't have a social life. That gave Craig an opportunity to creep back into my heart and into China's life. Whenever he came around, there was this unnatural, seemingly unbreakable connection. My feelings were caught up in a storm of emotions with no sense of direction. My heart went one way and my head went another. Yeah, it was crazy but that's what happened.

Still lurking in the wings, Marcus got wind of our reconnection. It was a hot summer weekend. As the sun rose, Marcus angrily banged on the door. His tone was violent.

"Open the darn door, dog!" the neighbors heard him scream.

It's a good thing the security latch was on. China slept on her cot, and Craig was inside too. Otherwise I might have gotten a serious beatdown from Marcus, the way he was clowning. Yeah, Craig had been staying over occasionally, and this happened to be one of those nights. I had no idea how much longer Craig could stand Marcus's screaming and banging on the door. Leaving Craig inside the apartment with China, I grabbed my crutches and hopped out the door to deal with that maniac. When Marcus saw me, he stood there laughing and stated, "Ha, how do you like the spell I put on you? Dog, screw me round, next time it'll be more than your foot."

Talking about his voodoo powers and how he'd worked his black magic, Marcus went on to say, "Baby, I told you I got the power! That's just the beginning of what I can do to you."

Marcus had always been a quick mover and shaker. This time, he moved so fast I barely knew what hit me. But it was his fist that went dead against my eye. Even with the throbbing pain, I went immediately into attack mode. That jerk wasn't getting away with this. I lifted my arms, brought down both crutches over his fat, round head, and cracked him as hard as I could. That cracking sound was so darn loud, I scared myself! Marcus quickly jumped over the handrail and ran through the corridor. This startled Craig, and he came dashing out of the apartment. When he saw that my eye was swollen big as a doorknob, his mouth dropped wide open.

"Man, I hate to see how swollen that dude was," he commented, looking at my banged up crutches.

As I hopped back inside, we laughed about that awesome ordeal. For the next two weeks, Craig continued to nurse me back to health.

It wasn't until I'd recovered that I heard the news about Mandy wanting to move out of her apartment.

When I asked her about the move, she said, "My lease is up and I ain't renewing. We've always lived southeast. It's time we moved to the southwest side of town."

With only two months left on my apartment lease, no way was I going to stay either. The timing was just right to venture out as well. Why not? I was used to packing up and relocating anyhow. And after all, she was the babysitter and my BFF. Mandy and I had worked hard to nurture our relationship, and I wasn't about to start over building another with some stranger. Moving to the other side of town wouldn't be a problem for work, either. The traffic flowed in the opposite direction, and I'd go from west to east. Mandy's new apartment was over by the 7700 block of Throop Street, and the apartment I found wasn't too far away—on the 7800 block of Loomis.

Even though we were no longer neighbors, China could still play with Cindy. China and Cindy played great as kids; we rarely had problems with them playing with their little toys. At times, Mandy gave them classwork to do—numbers, the alphabet, writing, reading, and coloring. We'd have a fresh start, and China would still have a playmate. Another exciting thing about this move: Craig had taken me over to a clinic right off 69th South Chicago Avenue, where we got our blood tested. Back in those days, this was something we needed for a marriage license. He'd gotten me one of those cheapo engagement rings. But we hadn't set a date or anything.

He said, "This marriage will be the start of our new beginning."

There we were in a new apartment as a family: me, Craig, and China. Yeah, the baby's daddy followed us there—and why not? We were engaged. China seemed so happy to have her father around. She even learned how to say "Dada." Before going to bed, she'd come to Craig with her arms open for a goodnight hug. The small things she did brought joy to my heart. China had always been a bright and intelligent child. She was now over two years old and could read and write. With us both working, she'd go to nursery school. The nursery school was right on 78th and Ashland. The fee they charged wasn't bad either; it was well worth the money. Sending China to nursery school made it better for Mandy. It gave her time to nurture her girls and allowed some time for herself.

When I came home from work, I could hardly wait to embrace China. This was when our mama time started. First, we hugged each other. As our arms locked, I would tell her, "I love you."

"Me you," she would reply.

I would tell her what my day had been like. When I asked about her day, she would say, "Me know colors, shapes, numbers, and ABCs. And teach us new story and rhyme, learn sharing toys, and playing together. I pick up so good and was the leader today. Mommy, school is a nice place." She spoke in a soft tone.

It did my heart wonders hearing her speak about school. I couldn't help but give her a smile and another hug.

"What will you wear to school tomorrow?" I would ask.

"My Winnie-Pooh dress with big bow and red white socks. Okay?" She'd smile.

"You're going to look real pretty tomorrow," I'd reply.

Once we had shared our day's activities, I would cook dinner, she would eat, take a bath, and we'd finish the day by reading one of her storybooks. Her favorite was *Goodnight Moon*. China read that one over and over. She'd even made up her own words while flipping the first few pages.

Once the story ended, she said in a sleepy voice, "Night stars, night air. Night noise everwhere."

I'd always smile just hearing her say *everwhere* instead of everywhere. 'Cause I knew then all lights went out.

After putting China down, Mandy and I got in our girl talk. Before our bodies shut down for the night, we'd speak on the phone and talk about some of everything. I learned Mandy slept with a butcher knife under her pillow. For her, it provided a feeling of security. For me, it was just one of the many things I knew about Mandy.

While I reminisced about some of the dramas in my life, she'd laugh without stopping or respond with disbelief.

"I have those 'you hurt me now, I'll get you back' moments," I told her.

Then I told her the story of the day Craig had gone out without me. It was a day when anger surfaced and would no longer stay suppressed. Talk about wacko—it gives the name a new height and meaning. The scene that followed was unimaginable, but it actually happened. When Craig went out, that was his big mistake. After he left, I went to the closet, took his clothes off the hangers, piled them in the middle of the floor, cut the lights, and struck a match to them. Then I sat in the dark and watched the bonfire.

In an instant, I had a Betty Broderick moment—just like when she set her man's clothes on fire. Or was it the Angela Bassett scene in *Waiting to Exhale*? Paying back her man was definitely a moment of rage.

Then again, maybe it was a Crystal Mangum moment. She's the Durham,

North Carolina, mother of three who was accused of setting her man's clothes on fire in a bathtub. In any case, each one of their actions made a clear statement: You hurt me, I'll hurt you back! So, really, those rising hormones aren't anything to mess with.

The fire was barely blazing when Craig returned. As he entered the room, our eyes slowly locked. He brushed by me to stomp out the fire. *(At this point, you may want to open your imagination for what followed—or think what you'd say if someone torched your clothes.)*

Craig yelled out, "You, you black b—! What the devil have you done, I could kick your . . ." When it was over, my actions made the statement: You tortured me; I'll torture you back.

As it happened, my mindset switched into fight or flight mode. It was the thought of his abandonment during my pregnancy and China's birth; his cruel words, his lying, and his cheating ways. Thinking of all the wrong and unjust things he'd done, and what he might do in the future. Just envisioning Craig scorched by those blazing flames—that was my state of mind in the moment.

Craig's clothing meant a lot to him. I assumed all the clothes burnt were Craig's. But the twist was that they weren't even his! Craig had been borrowing his brother Rondale's clothes. It's not a good thing when women have vengeful moments—but when we do, watch out! We'll go into a rage and retaliate. So, exactly how did Craig and Rondale resolve the clothes issue? Well, it was never discussed, at least not with me. Craig continued to hang out with the guys, though.

And I never committed that destructive act again. Still, I wondered: was I cursed to be a mirror of my dad's violent behavior? Maybe I was just unlucky in love? Or was it that I was destined to engage in toxic relationships?

In any case, we put the scene behind us. I revealed this incident to Mandy, but it would be the last time we'd reminisce about the past.

A tragedy ended the relationship with my dear Mandy. It happened early one morning. As the sun rose, we were awoken by someone at the door: *Knock! Knock! Knock!* I got up, grabbed my robe, quickly moved toward the door, and peered through the peephole. There stood two distinguished, well-dressed men, one African American and the other Caucasian. Judging from their appearances, these men could only bring bad news. Once I opened the door, I felt a sadness that hovered in the air.

The detectives wanted to make sure I was seated before telling me why they came. Sitting on the couch I wondered, *What could they possibly want with me?* It didn't take long to find out.

The African-American man stated, "We have some bad news. Your friend, Mandy, was murdered."

My hands shook as I cried out, "Oh my God, no, no!"

It took a while for me to compose myself. I wasn't able to speak, just to listen. "It must have happened sometime before daybreak since her kids were sleep. The little one, Cindy, found Mandy with the knife still in her throat."

"Oh my god!" I howled. "Where is Cindy now?"

He responded, "She's with relatives. Will you be okay if we continue?"

I told him, "Yeah, go ahead."

"She had over twenty stab wounds. We believe she knew her killer, since there was no forced entry."

I interjected and said, "Mandy always slept with a knife under her pillow."

He responded, "Well, that must be the one."

No one was a closer friend to Mandy than I. For this reason, I was expected to provide the answers to many questions. They interrogated me right there in my living room. "How long have you known Mandy? How close were you and Mandy? What type of relationship did she have with her estranged husband or boyfriend? How well do you know either of them? Who do you suspect as the killer?"

When it came to that question, I jumped in and said, "It's her estranged husband, Baylee, who probably done it."

The next four weeks were trying for us all.

For a week or two, China would ask, "Where's Manda and Cinda? Can I go see 'em?"

At a young age, death and tragedy are difficult to understand. By the second week, I'd gotten China to understand that Mandy had left and wasn't coming home, and that Cindy had to move away as well. Fern and Cindy both went to live with their aunt somewhere in the far west suburbs. With

Mandy gone, we had little contact with the girls. A lot of the time, I thought about my Mandy and the times we spent together with the kids. How deeply I missed her! I often wondered how those girls were doing. We later discovered Cindy had problems coping and needed professional help. Eventually, the culprit came forth and confessed. Go figure! All this time the murderer was in our circle. What a blow! I was right—it was Baylee! What possible motive was present for him to have committed this act? But what was most heartbreaking of all was leaving his children to grow up without either parent.

Even with a confession in hand, I was summoned as a witness for the prosecution. That was an ordeal I didn't want to face. When Dana and I entered the courtroom, it was terrifying. Baylee's family threatened to put me six feet under if I testified. There was a gang of 'em, at least eight. Their voices echoed no matter where we sat. The threats sounded loud—that's how bold they were.

They moved from the third row of seats to sit directly behind us, making sure we heard their threats.

"Let her open her mouth. She'll be dead," they said in harmony.

Maybe they wouldn't kill me. But I feared they'd actually go through with their threat. Wasn't nothing nice about his kinfolks; they meant business. It was fate that spared my life, 'cause Baylee was still getting psychiatric treatments. Since he was undergoing treatment, the trial was rescheduled. Of course, Baylee had pleaded insanity. So if there wasn't a trial, I didn't have to worry about getting killed—at least, not then. And to think, I'd get protection from the police as a safety measure—huh, not a chance!

Two months later, a county sheriff appeared at my apartment with another subpoena. I remembered how intimidated I was and the threats made against my life during the first court appearance.

So this time, I told a fib. And why not—it wasn't worth dying for, nor would it bring Mandy back from the grave.

Since the sheriff had never met me, I told him, "That must be the lady who once lived here."

I reeled him in, hook, line, and sinker. Well, maybe it wasn't a decent thing to have done, but Mandy was gone forever. Nothing anyone said could bring her back. My testimony would only give Mandy's killer a few months in a hospital, anyway, and we all know how that pans out. After so long, they're free to walk this earth.

Baylee was the bad guy here, but my conscience was working overtime carrying the lie that I had conjured up. At the time, my reasoning sounded justifiable. Although horrified and intimated by their threats, my actions were so low. Back then, boiling it down, I needed to have stepped up. And all my insides felt rotten to the core, to say the least. I struggled with my thoughts, knowing it wasn't about myself—the family needed closure. Whether my life was in danger or not, the simple solution was to have stepped up, or even pleaded the fifth out of fear. Not to have shown up at all—that action still weighs on my mind, unforgivable and irresponsible.

With all that happened, we continued to embrace Mandy's memory and cherish the relationship—leaving behind another shoe print along our journey.

The Insight

The experience of losing a friend is never easy:

- Allow time to grieve.
- Realize that the relationship was with someone special.
- Embrace the memory.
- Be patient with the process of all emotions.
- Take readjusting day by day.
- Open the doors to build new friendships.

CHAPTER FIVE

Dump Him Like It's Hot

After Mandy's death, we moved back to the southeast side of town. It was the winter of 1974; Craig found a beautiful three-bedroom high-rise apartment in Hyde Park, overlooking Lake Michigan. Our new apartment was right off Lake Shore Drive. The complex was called the 50/50 Building. When Renna told Craig that their oldest daughter, Little Barbie, was coming to live with us, I had no problem embracing her. Little Barbie was already seven years old. This was a good move 'cause China needed another female figure in her life. Even as a big sister, Little Barbie was a great playmate for China. She'd walk her to school. The school she went to was not that far from China's preschool.

It was obvious China loved her big sister. She'd offer Little Barbie her toys; she never was a selfish child. She had a whole trunk of toys and books and didn't mind sharing. There were Raggedy Ann and Barbie dolls, a tricycle, tea sets, a slinky, blocks, peg boards, puzzles, Fisher Price stuff, a Rubik's Cube, tons of stuffed animals, board games, a toy phone and vacuum cleaner, a huge collection of storybooks, an Easy Bake oven, and some of everything else. Before she had a playmate, she'd had imaginary friends or dolls—at tea parties, sipping and chatting, or bathing and feeding them. Sometimes she'd even read to them.

When she wasn't playing with imaginary people or dolls, I would play with her.

"Ring, ring." She picked up her toy phone and said, "Fo' yew, Mommy."

"Hello there," I answered. "She told me you were calling today. Well, didn't tell me that one. Yes, I'll be here. You wanna talk back to her? Okay, then."

I handed the phone back, and she took her pink phone into the bedroom and chatted away.

When it came to those imaginary friends, I had to play it all the way—better not disappoint her. It was lots of fun watching her face light up as I spoke on the phone. *Amazing how kids can learn to entertain themselves*, I thought.

China had a habit of calling her sister Baba. Sometimes you didn't know what she was saying, Dada or Baba. In her soft voice, both names sounded similar. When it was time to go beddy-bye, Baba would have to follow. It was a thrill seeing the two of them together. Outside, they'd throw snowballs or build a snowman. They'd decide whose hat the snowman should wear, Little Barbie's or China's. Inside, they'd scatter toys about and play dress up. That was a sight, seeing the girls walk in heels, wearing plastic makeup and shedding feathers throughout the house. My hands were full caring for those two, but I loved every minute.

Since my relationship with Craig had been shaky, I was cautious about bonding with Little Barbie. She had already been torn from one broken home, but we'd formed a new blended family. No one ever said step-parenting was easy. Allowing our relationship to take its natural course was a slow process. It wasn't about finding an instant connection; our bonding would happen over time. It made me feel good to open my heart to nurture our relationship. As we grew closer, I looked forward to activities together, such as taking walks, bike riding, going on special outings, going shopping, and being supportive at her school events. It all came down to building trust and respect, to develop a warm and involved relationship.

But no matter how I tried to hold the family together, it wasn't enough. Craig was destined to be unfaithful. Getting married meant nothing to him. Craig should've had the sense not to give out our phone number to his new mistress. His affairs hit home, and this one in particular broke our relationship.

It all happened while Craig and I gathered in the bedroom around the candlelight. As we prepared for dinner, my mind drifted and I thought, *This is going to be an enchanting evening.*

Before I'd finished setting the table, going back and forth from kitchen to bedroom, the phone rang. It was another woman.

I fumed, *She has some nerve calling here.*

When I answered, she asked, "Is this the lady of the house?"

(Here again, you may want to broaden your imagination for what follows.)

"Yeah, this is she," I replied.

"You black b—. I'm screwing your man. And I'm on my way to . . ." his mistress told me.

Who was she? I knew nothing of her, but she knew about me. Yep, Craig had betrayed us! Talk about anger to the umpteenth degree—I saw red, blood, sweat, and tears. I wanted to hurt them both.

When I returned to the room, I stood in the doorway, staring at his face. He asked, "Honey, who was that?"

Little did he know that his voice was the last thing I wanted to hear. When I got mad, I was nothing nice. Struck by anger, I turned, picked up the lamp, and threw it at him. He ducked, jumped up from the table, and followed me into the kitchen. That was another big mistake. I looked at the chicken frying over a sizzling hot flame, quickly grabbed the cast-iron skillet, and threw it at him. When he saw his food flying across the room he ducked, and it landed smack against the white walls. As tears flowed down my face, I told him about my conversation with his mistress. What happened afterward was similar to the famous Al Green melodrama—but without the grits. Or possibly it was a moment from the *Diary of a Mad Black Woman*, with me portraying Helen McCarter's character. Regardless of the scene, it became one of those mirthless evenings, particularly for Craig.

"I dare you to close one eye!" I screamed. "If you want to see tomorrow, it wouldn't be wise."

I paced from the living room to the bedroom with a knife in each hand, waiting for his mistress to appear at our door. All through the night, I stared at the door, hoping she'd come. Each time I crept into the bedroom, Craig sprung up like a spring.

He yelled, "I ain't asleep!"

No doubt Craig thought he was about to draw his last breath.

That whole event was completely mind-boggling. A rush of electrifying combat adrenaline had taken over. It felt like one of those out-of-body experiences. To have had discovered this level of anger inside me was beyond frightening. Having the capacity to kill in the spur of the moment scared me out of my wits. Recognizing this toxic, killer emotion in me and knowing that someone had pushed me to that degree was a rude awakening. That awareness made me realize the full volatility of our toxic relationship. Remorseful, embarrassed, and ashamed of my actions, my self-esteem had been diminished. It made me feel sick to stoop so low as to want to kill a human being.

To add fuel to the fire, Craig hit me with the news that he was still married. To have fabricated such a downright lie—saying he was divorced and proposing to me—was totally scandalous, completely out the box, and it hurt something awful. Yeah, he added salt to the wound!

There's one thing to be said: my baby's daddy was some kind of sicko person.

Had Craig wanted the best of both worlds so badly that he'd gone that far to deceive me again? Don't know what made me believe our relationship would be different. In a twisted kind of way, I wanted to believe he'd changed and our toxicity was nonexistent. But when Craig betrayed his marital vows, it was a sign of his true character. That's just the way he was! Obviously, Craig had no morals, catting about with the ladies. His actions attested to the fact that he was a cad. There was no doubt about his character—once a liar and cheater, you're bound to those lying, cheating traits. I saw him as a snake, his lies slithering from his tongue.

I found out his new mistress was one of the tellers where we banked at the Hyde Park Bank & Trust. I don't recall her name, and frankly cared even less how their relationship started. But I was willing to bet that he hit on her first and it blossomed from there. Make no mistake: when someone shows who they really are, believe them. Craig was definitely not marriage material. He cheated on his wife with me, was deceitful in make-believing he was single a second time, and then creepin' on me with the bank teller! The pattern spoke for itself—he was back full circle and one sick dude. When you've dealt with drama to that degree, it's time to give one another space. So the time to drop him like a hot potato had arrived. I'd come to face reality. Craig knew he'd screwed up royally. It was clear where we stood. The relationship had ended for good. We both shared a feeling of hurt—him for everything he'd said and done, me for acting out and being foolish enough to have trusted him. My act of violence proved to be a stone giveaway that I was my daddy's child.

I spent the next two weeks gathering empty boxes and looking for our own place. I'd found a one-bedroom apartment that was perfect for China and me. Once we split up, Craig took Little Barbie and went back to Renna. This was something I'd feared for Little Barbie—being involved in another breakup. So it was best that I had tiptoed to gain her trust, since I was no longer a part of her life. With Craig gone, I knew I had to provide the best for China and pursue my search to find that true relationship. I continued my job at the hospital and started college. I felt attending school would help close the gap.

It's time to step back and reflect on another moment of epiphany. I tried to give China everything her little heart desired. Craig never fully made an effort to embrace China within his paternal circle. Although Craig came from a huge family, his daughter was treated as an outcast. One thing for certain, he rarely brought her around his kinfolk.

Drifting from one apartment to the next, it was as if China and I were Gypsies. I'd finally gotten another chance to take the federal exam. I don't recall the exact score I tested at, but it was in the upper 90s. This time I took the job, a position as clerk. I continued with both jobs and attended college for about a year. While driving to my new job one day, I fell asleep at the wheel and almost rammed into a viaduct. The car had suddenly stopped, as if it had applied the brakes itself. My life flashed before my eyes, and I knew my guardian angel had woken me to see it all. After my near-death incident, I realized I needed to give up something: either working two jobs or going to school. So I quit my job at the University of Chicago Hospital. It wasn't a difficult choice, 'cause working two full-time jobs and going to school was a bit much. I really didn't have a social life either. Life revolved around working, college, and caring for China. She was my world, and I loved her deeply.

The next three years for us were encouraging. China was doing extremely well in school. She was at the top of her class. I had changed job positions and was finally making good money. Craig's promise to pay me child support was just words: a promise with no action.

There were months I'd get something and others I wouldn't see a dime. His debts were growing faster than I could add up, but I wasn't letting him get by without taking care of his parental responsibilities. Obviously, Craig had a problem with this. So there we were, back in court. Nope, I wasn't going to let him underpay or refuse to pay outright. Craig really wasn't happy, nor could he do anything about it.

I was pleased when the judge said, "I'm granting you an increase. We'll set it up for the money to come through the courts before it goes to you."

After our day in court, we continued to go our separate ways. Craig was with Renna trying to mend their relationship, and I was trying to build my family relationship.

The Insight

An intimate relationship with a married man can be extremely toxic. There are reasons on both sides not to engage in this type of relationship:

- The character of a person lessens.
- Once a cheater, always a cheater.
- The guilt.
- What you have is a borrowed relationship.
- Think about your future versus the other person's.
- Cheating is a sign of being untrustworthy and disrespectful.
- It shows an inability to commit.
- You'll always be considered the other woman.

CHAPTER SIX

Wedding Bells

China and I went it alone and moved again. On the southeast side, we found a cute two-bedroom apartment on 83rd and Avalon. It was small, but China would have her own space and so would I. That's what mattered! Even though I was still going to school and working, I managed to find some time for socializing. When one of our relatives passed, I went to his/her homecoming. While I was there, I met Mike Crawford. Mike was a friend of one of my older cousins. It just so happened that I sat next to her at the funeral. For her telling me about Mike, I barely heard the services.

Leaning over my shoulder, she'd whispered, "Cuz, got someone I'd like you to meet. His name is Mike, he's divorced, and he's looking for a nice person. You know, I thought of you, cuz."

"Okay, but I'm trying to pay attention. How about we talk later?" I whispered, just to keep her silent.

At the repast Mike approached me. "Hi there, I'm Mike. You must be the lovely lady I've heard so much about. And it's all good now."

Mike had two ex-wives, was twice my age, and stood about five foot seven. His hair was black and gray (particularly his sideburns), and he had a medium-toned complexion. He wore black, rectangular glasses which contrasted with his oblong-shaped face. Many of his front teeth were missing, so he had a mouth full of gums. He wasn't a looker, that's for sure. Another thing, his outfits left a lot to be desired. That brown and beige checkered suit he sported had faded out of fashion many years ago.

We exchanged numbers, dated for eight months, and got engaged. I can't recall every detail that attracted me to Mike; for sure, it wasn't his looks. Despite being toothless and tasteless in fashion, he made up for it with his pleasing smile, sense of humor, thoughtfulness, genuine religious attitude, and his great affection for us both. Seemingly, he was an all-around nice guy. And we had a lot in common. We even started going to his church. He had a degree in music, and had gotten a part-time job playing the piano at church. Not only was he a musician, he had a strong testimony for the gospel. He also served as a Bible school teacher. On Sunday mornings and Bible study evenings, China loved hearing him teach the Word. During his teachings, it was evident he was well-loved by all the kids. He was a gospel scholar, and he'd always quote from the Scripture, even around just the three of us. A man of religious values was a man after my own heart.

We spent Friday nights at the roller rink. I wasn't much of a skater—I was constantly falling to the ground. When Mike saw China geared up with kneepads and all, he hit that rink to roll with her. They took off in a squatting position. Alternating their feet—right, then left—away they went, ripping around corners and bouncing to the music. As they glided around the rink, it was comforting to see that big smile on her face.

Mike wasn't just a skater; he had a knack for cooking, too. I wasn't much of a cook, but Mike could prepare delicious meals. Don't quite remember a specific one, but I knew they were better than any meal I'd ever fixed. And every time we ate, he made sure there was candlelight and wine. He didn't have much money, but gave everything of himself. In the gift department, he was always thoughtful, showering us with presents.

Whenever I told him I was going shopping with China, he'd ask if he could go with us.

"Sure," I'd answer. I never knew which of us he'd choose to spring a gift on.

He was a passionate kisser, and he was always all over me. He loved being touchy-feely. When we walked, it was hand in hand. He liked snuggling as we sat on the couch, and he even hugged me whenever we'd part. When he wasn't spending time with us, he was out on the courts. He loved sports and played tennis well. He looked rather cute with his little outfit as he chased and swung at those tennis balls. He was a master at it and could kick some butt. Enthusiastically, I'd yell out, "Baby, that's the way to go!" He'd always turn to look at me with one of those loving smiles.

In all that time we were together, there was no intimacy, just admiration and wanting to rectify my guilt. Yeah, I'd acquired a feeling of guilt from the day I gave birth out of wedlock on this God-forsaken earth.

I need a man to be complete, were the words that clung to my mind.

Perhaps it's difficult for any of you to understand where I'm coming from with that thought. Just know, the more those words gnawed at me, the more my stomach churned. And that churning crept up on the left and right side of my stomach. I knew it came from just thinking about what I'd had to endure, being a single parent and going it alone. I'd carried a heavy burden all those years, knowing my daughter lacked so much in life by not having a daddy. And that's not what I wanted for her. She deserved way more than what I'd given her.

I took on a mission to find Mr. Right, looking to build a family unit. Now, my mission had finally run its course. Okay, it might have been a sick way of thinking and acting on my part. But I'm not one to give up easily. I'm a determined person, and I was determined to provide a two-parent home. Perhaps I'm best described as unpredictable or "out there." Yup, I'll follow a different path from everyone else. You probably wouldn't have an intimate relationship with a married man. I've done that! You probably wouldn't have a child out of wedlock. I've done that! You probably wouldn't engage in shacking up. I've done that! You probably wouldn't set your man's clothes on fire. I've done that! You'd probably look for love first before acting on a relationship. I don't have to! I just jump into it and give it my best. Nah, that's not a drastic move, but a sacrifice, and one I'd make to offer a good life for my daughter.

With Mike in our lives, he'd be that person. I thought of him as our savior, my hero, my hubby, and a daddy for China. Mike was the kinda person I could easily love for life. Our relationship definitely wouldn't be one-sided, either. With his fine qualities, he'd already sparked my love bone. So when he proposed, I was bursting with joy. Yes, indeed, I was so full of happiness and ready to explode wide open. His proposal came at an unexpected moment.

The three of us had gone to a Service Merchandise store. Having walked the aisles and taken the slips over to a cashier to check out, we watched our items as they rolled down the conveyor belt. We had gotten some good stuff for home and a toy or two for China. I thought our shopping trip was over, but it wasn't.

"Honey, let's walk over by the jewelry counter. I want the two of you to see this ring," Mike said, without hesitating.

"Okay, why not? It's on our way out," I responded.

I saw nothing unusual about his request. Mike loved jewelry. He had plenty of gold and silver chains and rings. So what was one more for his collection?

At the counter, Mike spoke with the sales rep. "Yes, I'm back. I'll take that ring now," he told her.

She reached inside the glass case. My eyes widened and my brows rose. I was totally surprised to see her pull out a diamond ring for a woman. The engagement setting was oval-shaped with diamond side stones that added sparkle. As he looked down at China with a big smile, Mike turned and looked at me.

Taking hold of my right hand, he said, "You've brought me joy and happiness. I can't imagine spending my life without the two of you. Honey, will you take me as your husband?"

I took a deep breath, and exclaimed, "Oh my goodness!" After the initial shock, I placed my hands on his cheeks, gently pulled his face to mine, and gave him one of the juiciest smacks right on his lips—and didn't care who saw.

As he went to place the ring on my finger, the yeses came out. "Yes, yes. I will marry you," I told him.

The way Mike proposed was pretty darn romantic. We chose November 3, 1983, as our date to tie the knot.

After my lease ran out, China and I moved again. This time, there would be wedding bells in our life. There was a vacancy at a building down from Cedar Park Cemetery, right off 125th and Halsted. That area was decent: no gangs, and the complex was a mix of Caucasians and African Americans. The marriage wouldn't be easy for China to swallow, because Mike wasn't her father.

Weeks before the wedding, I'd learned some valuable news from Dana. "I'll run away from home if Mom marries him," China had told my sister. "Auntie, I want her to marry my dad."

After finding that out, I figured it was time to set the record straight.

I told China, "Baby, I love you. I won't ever let anyone take that love. So if Mommy gets married, you'll have a dad. And that's double the love for you."

"But I already have a dad," China replied in a soft voice.

"Mama's got to have a serious talk with her baby," I told her. "Naw baby, you have a father, not a dad. There's a difference. Any man can be a father through sexual actions and conception. But a dad, he'll put nothing before you. You're his priority. Dads, they spend time with you. They give purpose to your life. They teach you life lessons. Not only do they care financially, but emotionally. You'll connect in heart and soul. Baby, that's the kind of dad you deserve. You're one of the reasons Mommy does what she does. I love you, baby."

She nodded and replied, "Okay, Mommy. I love you too."

China had always been a great listener. Just by her response, I knew she'd understood the message.

After our little mother-daughter talk, we gave each other a big bear hug.

Our wedding day happened as planned. Although it took twelve years, I'd found a soul mate. Mike was the reflection of my soul, and vice versa. China was twelve years old when we were finally going to have a nuclear family. This wasn't a dress rehearsal; it was real. After working a half-day, we held our wedding at the apartment. The only decorations were the beige, white, and lavender helium balloons that read, "Congratulations! You're Newlyweds!" I wore a cream-colored satin A-line dress with lace layered around the collar. Its wide bow sash added a special touch to the dress. Otherwise, there was really nothing fancy about it. I had on small diamond stud earrings. My makeup was set, and I had applied a shiny chocolate lip gloss. The gloss made my lips look kissable.

Since I didn't have a veil, I placed some baby's breath through my hair.

I brought China a princess-style dress in a satiny lavender color, with an overlay of white lace and a fancy sash. With her dark bangs and hair up in a ball with baby's breath tucked in, she looked like a princess. She wore white lace tights and lavender shoes. She even had on a soft-colored lipstick and pearl earrings. Mike had on his black suit with a beige shirt, lavender tie, and matching hankie that was tucked into his pocket. He was all decked out with polished black patent leather shoes.

Including the minister, there was an audience of around thirty family members and friends to witness our special day. We were all crammed inside the small two-bedroom apartment in Calumet Park.

China slowly scattered flower petals as she walked down the aisle. The start of the Stevie Wonder song "Ribbon in the Sky" was my cue to come out of the bedroom. As the music played, I gracefully walked to meet my husband-to-be. As I passed through the crowd, I turned to sneak my mom a smile. All of a sudden, I felt an eerie sensation, as if Daddy was alongside me. Even after his death, the loss of our relationship had been difficult to accept. I felt abandoned, and I missed him so badly. And this day was the hardest.

I quickly shook away the feeling and regrouped. It was bad enough that my right foot twisted over as I walked. Then my makeup started to smear, since I'd started tearing up. Once Mike and I stood at the altar, hand in hand, my palms began dripping with sweat. I felt a bunch of different emotions—excitement, nervousness, and happiness—all at once. The slight squeeze I'd gotten from Mike's hand assured me it was going to be okay. After the minister gave his traditional marriage spiel, we recited our vows.

Mike's endearing message touched my heart: "I knew you were the woman for me the moment I saw you. I love you and yours very much. I want to share my life with you both. On this day, I promise to shower you with love. I promise to give you an abundance of joy. I promise to bring you happiness. I promise to grow with you in mind, body, and spirit. I promise to be your protector and keep our family safe. I promise to love you for eternity."

After hearing his spoken message, I'd hoped to pass along my love: "I've grown to embrace your warmth and cherish your love. On this day, we will unite, be as one. I offer you these solemn vows. I vow to be truthful. I vow to respect you. I vow to be honest and open. I vow to grow with you and fall in love more each day. I'm honored to be your wife. And know I, too, do love you."

After sharing our vows, the rest of the night was spent enjoying the festivities.

There was no doubt about our relationship, 'cause I'd finally done it. My thoughts celebrated: *I's a married woman now!*

Gosh, those were some beautiful words. *I's a married woman.* Just as it so easily expressed how Shug felt in the story *The Color Purple.*

To begin our marriage in style, we decided to purchase a home. We looked at a gorgeous three-bedroom, tri-level brick house in the far suburbs of Markham. The moment we saw this place, we knew it was right. Matter of fact, the house was owned by the finance director who worked at my job. He was practically giving it away for a steal. The place was fabulous, with all kinds of quaint features. Picture this: high cathedral ceilings, a winding staircase, a built-in skylight, breakfast nook, fireplace, beautiful wooden floors throughout, enclosed glass patio, three bedrooms, two-and-a-half bathrooms, a basement with a wet bar, a workshop area, piped-in music/intercom system, a big backyard for China to play in, and a two-car garage. As first-time homeowners, this house was perfect for us. Mike was sold once he saw the huge workshop area. Being pretty good with his hands, he loved to build custom-made furnishings. It would be just the thing he needed to create his furniture.

Our neighbors, Arlene and Michael, were a much younger couple. Arlene was short with a pretty chocolate complexion, and she wore her thick black hair Jheri-curled. Michael was of average height, light skinned with a few acne blotches, and a little on the heavy side. They both appeared to be in their mid-twenties and had been married for three years already. Arlene had just delivered a baby boy.

We had several months of bliss as a happily married couple, but that soon changed. Despite my hopes and dreams for a fulfilled marriage, it was held together by a thread. What was once our formula for wedded bliss soon vanished. I wanted our marriage to work. Every single vow I'd taken, I meant! I'd expected it to last *until death do us part*, and for China to have a daddy for eternity.

In the first two months, we took pride in decorating our new home together. We attended social functions, had dinner gatherings at the house, and entertained family and friends by throwing card parties. Even our intimate moments were electrifying. Once our relationship faltered, I had to accept that the honeymoon was over. Within six months, the man I'd married and fallen in love with had gotten beside himself. It started when I convinced him to get dental work. Strangely, I'd wound up creating a monster. He stopped helping pay the bills, and all the money had dwindled from our account. Mike even changed his whole appearance; he'd gone from wearing plaid or checked suit jackets to smarter solid colors. He'd given up wearing shirts with wide collars and wore straight, pointed ones, trying to look more suave.

He stopped greeting me warmly—not a single "good morning," "hello," or "goodbye." He stopped referring to me with terms of endearment; the days of "honey," "dear," and "darling" were far behind, as were little things like "Good morning, dear," "I love you," or "Honey, how was your day?" When it came to affection, I no longer received any of his gentle, cozy hugs or passionate kisses. He wasn't showing sexual interest, either. There was silence in our bedroom; he slept on his side and I on mine. He had no problem falling asleep, while I'd lay awake wondering how we'd gone awry. Early on, we'd pressed our naked bodies together just to feel the warmth. With my head resting on his chest, we cuddled with his legs interlocked with mine. His watery kisses soothed me to sleep.

He suddenly changed his Fruit of the Loom briefs to new sexy bottoms— and he wasn't wearing them for me. He hung out later than usual. We had little communication, but he'd seem to be in a good mood. When he was home, he'd shut himself in his den and talked on the phone as the music played in the background. We'd stopped having meals together; he'd eat at one time and China and I at another. It was so hurtful, sad, and lonely.

No doubt, there had to have been some infidelity. The voice at the end of the phantom phone calls only spoke when Mike answered. This was a sure sign of him having another woman. I'd trusted and believed in those promises he'd made, but I felt the wrath of his betrayal and abandonment. It felt just like being abandoned by Dad after his death. And I couldn't forget the abandonment by Craig after he'd gotten me pregnant. He'd told me, "You're my woman and I'm your man." He'd convinced me he was committed. Still, I'd taken him back only to get dumped again.

Oh boy, can you pick 'em! crossed my mind.

To my surprise, China found a diary Mike had kept from the day we wed.

She came to me and said, "Mommy, look what I found. It's a diary all about you. I found it."

I never got the full details about where China had discovered the diary. It was either under the bar in the basement or in his office den. Anyhow, wherever it was found, it was a blessing! Once I looked, it showed that Mike zeroed in on my every move. It was frightening to learn my every move was being scrutinized. To see the diary full of entries chilled me to the bone. The notes Mike made showed my leaving date and time, where I'd gone, with whom (if anybody), and the time I'd returned.

10 a.m. / Sat, 4-14-1984 / She went to the mall / Gone with Peaches / 8:15 p.m. brought back two bags

7 a.m. / Mon, 4-16-1984 / Left for work / Carpooling / 7 p.m. arrived home late – why?

It was a scary feeling knowing my moves were being tracked. The time had come to rescue us from this monster. As much as I wanted China to have a dad, we weren't going to stay trapped in a toxic marriage. Although our little family would cease to exist, I needed some peace of mind.

Not only was I cursed with Dad's traits, but Mom's as well. Mom couldn't pick out a good man, and neither could I. I never failed at picking the wrong guy to love. While looking for Mr. Right, all I found was Mr. Wrong.

We were sleeping in the same bed but far apart. He was totally on one side, with me all the way on the other. With our romance gone, there was nothing Mike wouldn't attempt. There was one episode that showed how wicked-minded he could be.

Returning home from a business trip, I couldn't get into the house. I tried one lock after another without success. Finally, there was no other way but to break a window and put China through it. Once she was inside, that's when we found out Mike had changed the locks. That was the last straw. I burst into tears and prayed to God to show us the way. I was kneeling on my knees right beside the winding staircase, with my head lifted up toward the cathedral ceiling. As tears flowed down my cheeks, I pleaded for guidance. To my disbelief, a cloudy shadow spirit appeared at the head of the staircase.

In a deep baritone voice, it spoke to me. "LEAVE and I'll be with you." The cloudy shadow faded, and my tears began to return from whence they came. I felt as though a burden had lifted from my shoulders. I had never encountered such a feeling. Afterward, I stood up straight and tall, feeling like a new person emerging to life. The figure that had appeared before me could only been our Heavenly Father. No doubt—I'd fully experienced His presence.

After hearing the Holy voice, I knew China and I were well-protected. God had told me to leave, and that became all the faith I needed. We were going to be watched over. As I passed in and out of a relationship, our guardian angel would guide us through the journey. Packing only a few items, we left. We moved back home with Mom.

I told Mike, "I'm leaving you. I'll be back this weekend to gather the rest of our things."

With a smirk, Mike replied, "Don't you think we need to talk about it? Are we getting a divorce or separation?"

Personally, I wanted nothing more from our marriage, not even the memories. Mike gloated over what he'd done to us with a grin plastered across his face. He wanted the house and whatever else he felt entitled to. But the only things he'd brought to this marriage were his homemade pieces. Mike was a security officer. To supplement his salary, he played the organ at church. If it weren't for my income, we'd never have qualified for the loan. At the time we bought the house, it was $58,000, and the buyer had to make at least half of what the house cost. So the financing was based on my income. Anyhow, that was what the realtor said.

When Dana and I returned to pick up our furniture and clothes, Mike wouldn't let us in. I knocked on the door four times.

He finally yelled out, "What you want!"

I thought, *No way is this gonna fly.*

He opened the door slightly.

"You better—you better not even go there," I said. As we elbowed our way in, he quickly grabbed the phone and called the police.

Dana snatched the phone, ripped it off the wall, lowered her hammer, and said, "I'm about to take this hammer and smash all your homemade furniture." You see, my sister didn't care too much for him anyway, and she wasn't one you wanted to mess with. She'd come in with a weapon and was prepared to take care of business at any cost.

Moments later, they were tussling back and forth. Mike dashed through the door with blood dripping from his body.

"Help me! Someone please help me, call the police!" he shouted, as he ran down the street banging on the neighbors' doors.

Dana yelled out, "Go get the other hammer from the car. Hurry! Hurry!"

When Dana finally caught up with Mike, he was pleading for a neighbor to help him. (And no, it wasn't Arlene or Michael.) He had made it all the way down to the neighbors' house at the end of the block. Dana grabbed the glasses from his face, threw them on the ground, crushed them with her foot, and started to reach toward his lips.

Dana yelled, "Give my sister back those false teeth she bought you!" She tried to rip them right from his mouth.

I cried out, "No, Sis! Stop, I don't want his used teeth!"

Just then, the police arrived.

While I explained, Mike screamed out, "I want 'em locked up! Both of 'em—lock 'em up."

"Darn it, I don't know who to take to jail, all you nigs bleeding," the po-po said, not hesitating. Yep, I was bleeding too. While the police waited, we were able to get our belongings. After that episode, Mike was known in our neighborhood as Mike the Wimp. China and I left the house, leaving Mike with his shabby homemade pieces. They were the only things he'd brought to the marriage. We left behind our imprint, making another shoe print. No doubt our relationship was over, along with any chance of giving China a dad.

The Insight

In a toxic marital relationship, see it for what it's worth:

- Don't become codependent. Be willing to leave a toxic relationship.
- Don't be blinded by feelings. Recognize they cripple a pure marriage.
- Avoid unsafe environments. Self-esteem is decreased and energy becomes drained.

CHAPTER SEVEN

Splitting Up—And Taking Snapshots

Moving in with Mom and the family was no picnic. Luckily for us we didn't stay long—only three months. After that move, I made three solemn pledges: 1) never to return, 2) to make it on my own, and 3) to have little to no contact with Mom. That third commitment had been my biggie, trying to keep distance from Mom. But it needed to be done, 'cause I'd brought on too much drama. I'd been too bogged down with my own issues. I'd struggled to raise China in and out of those toxic relationships, along with my other crazy, raggedy decisions. No way did Mom need any more of my drama.

I told Mom before leaving, "You won't hear from me, but don't worry. Concentrate on the others. I'm a fighter and I'll make it. You've always said I was my daddy's child."

It had become hard, but whenever I'd made a promise, I'd stuck to it. That's just how I was.

With the help of Peaches, we found a rental home. Our new place was a lovely two-bedroom gray and white house. We used the enclosed back porch as a sitting area. This cute little house was right in Harvey. The landlord charged $430 a month for rent. It wasn't much at first sight, but Peaches pumped me up, knowing I had a knack for decorating.

She always told me, "You can take a shack and make it look like a million-dollar home."

Yeah, guess I did have a knack for fixing up a place. Anyhow, by now I was willing to accept just about any place to live. China's school was only three blocks away. When it started in September, she'd attend her freshman year at Thornton Township High School. It was the same school I had graduated from. We were ready to settle into our new home a month before school began.

Mike and I still had some unfinished business. He was playing hardball, refusing to give me a divorce. Each time we went to court, he'd contest the divorce. So I stopped the petition and waited it out. Many scars had to heal before I could move on with a social life. I had no hunger to spend an evening with another man. The only energy I could muster up was spent on going to work, going to school, and spending quality time with China, hoping to smooth over the bad choices I'd made in our lives.

China was thirteen years old and had become a teenager. She found many adult topics to discuss. If you stop to think about it, our children do ask lots of questions. Their brains are like sponges. Perhaps that's how their little minds mature. Some of China's questions had been about puberty; others sort of caught me off guard.

"How did you and my father meet? Why didn't you two get married? Why do you think he doesn't spend time with me?" She asked in her soft voice.

I can't quite remember every answer I gave. But when we talked, a glow of life gleamed through her. With her vigor and charm, China was truly someone special—the center of my universe. China had become a teenager. Unbelievable, how quickly they pass through each stage of life! It's as though we parents need to freeze each frame, to savor those Kodak moments.

Again, it's time to step back and reflect on a moment of epiphany.

There's another defining period in life. Those tender, growing years from five to six to seven to eight to nine to ten—and so on.

At around five years old, China would ride the public bus. Once Little Barbie went back home, she'd take the bus to the Hyde Park Neighborhood Club before going to her pre-K programs. She even knew where to stand and wait for the bus. She'd read the schedule to find out which number bus she needed to get on. After reading the street signs, she knew exactly where to get off. Now, how smart was that for such a youngster?

She was active in her after-school programs. At the YMCA, China took karate lessons where she'd wear her little three-piece karate gi uniform with its black sash wrapped around her tiny waist. China became excellent at it and won an award.

As a parent, that was something to be proud of. Boy, she wouldn't be a person to mess with either!

On alternate days, at the YMCA, China participated in ballet lessons. Wearing her little tutu with soft, pink, satin-ribbon shoes, she became quite a skilled ballerina. This was another one of the activities she'd grown to love and master.

On special occasions, particularly birthdays and Christmas, China would sit by the window, looking out. As the clock ticked away from 5:30 p.m. to 6:30 p.m. to 7:30 p.m. to 8:30 p.m. to 9:30 p.m., she waited and longed for her father to arrive bearing gifts—gifts he'd promised he'd bring. His absence would leave China with a full day of disappointment.

At around six years old, although China had toys of her own, she didn't have Chinese checkers. But that was no cause for her to do what she did. Anyhow, it was done! She'd stolen the game from school and brought it home to tuck away with her other toys. But she was honest about it. When I found out, China agreed to take it back and apologize to her teacher and classmates. Nothing of this sort happened again. She wasn't a bad child—just doing kiddy things!

At seven years old China learned to entertain herself. She liked to play outdoors a lot. It didn't matter whether there was anyone to play with. She had lots of books and loved to read them as well, inside or outside. If she wasn't outdoors riding her bike or reading books, China found something else to keep herself amused. That was quite impressive for a single child.

At eight years old, China was a bright student. Her teachers felt that she was smart enough to go to the University of Chicago Laboratory School. This was not a coincidence, either, because they made the same request the following year. Even though China was a gifted student, I chose to keep her in a regular class environment on both occasions. It did make me proud, though.

While Craig showed her no love, it was her Uncle Rondale who embraced her with a memorable trip when she was eight years old.

After knocking at the door, he said, "We're having a family reunion. Can I take her to Georgia? Don't worry about the money, I'm paying for everything."

When I looked down at China, her eyes lit up and she had the biggest smile on her face. "Can I go, Mommy, can I, please?" she asked.

There was no way I could refuse this offer. The trip would last five days. No doubt Rondale stood to be a better man than his brother Craig would ever be. Rondale was a great man to recognize China as part of his family circle. He was a firm believer that children should always grow up knowing their kinfolk. For her, this trip was a most memorable five days.

At nine, China already had a love for shopping. One of her favorite pastimes was going to shopping malls and picking out designer clothes. Her favorite place to shop was on State Street and Michigan Avenue. She loved to shop at Sears, Marshall Field's, Carson Pirie Scott, J. C. Penney, and I. Magnin. Even at this age, she didn't like shopping at what we called "cheap stores." I couldn't get her to wear a pair of shoes from Payless or Community Discount Store, but don't think I didn't try.

China wasn't much interested in wearing dresses. She loved her pant sets and miniskirts. She'd come into the room wearing her miniskirt with a pair of her favorite black knee-high suede boots and a matching black felt hat, accessorized with her gold or silver wide-hooped earrings. It was such a funny sight to see those little skinny legs inside those wide boots. Every time she wore them over at my friend Dawn's house, we'd burst into laughter seeing her stick-like legs inside those high boots. We called them her "Lady of the Night" boots. Really, you'd have to have been there to appreciate our laughter. It was obvious that by that age, China had found a taste for fashion. She was our little fashion diva.

At ten, China had a knack for hooking up equipment, whether it was a TV stand, an entertainment center set, or a phonographic stand (and there wasn't a screw, nut, or bolt left out). She'd master each task without even reading the instructions. All China had to do was look at the diagram or picture from the packaging. I was never worried about buying anything that needed to be assembled. She was gifted and talented, and this was a prime example of her skills at an early age.

At eleven, she started cooking. It started the time I really made a bad meal. I can't quite remember what the dish was, though. But it doesn't matter, 'cause it must not have looked nor tasted edible.

China asked, "Mom, what the devil is that? I know you can't think I'm eating it!"

Guess I probably should have been insulted but I wasn't. Afterward, China took control of making the meals. What a great cook she became! It took her no time to figure out our meals for the week. She'd thaw out the meat before she'd leave for school so she knew exactly what to cook for the evening. And that's how she became our little Suzy Homemaker.

At twelve, China could communicate with the hearing impaired. This was a skill she taught herself by reading and studying sign language books. China used her skills and knowledge to teach others as well. Often, we communicated with one another this way just to stay abreast of the language. China was really advanced at this—and self-taught!

Although she was in her early teens (I don't recall the exact age), China slept with me off and on (more on than off). Some may have felt that was awkward, but I didn't think our sleeping arrangements were unwholesome in any way. I'd gotten a full-sized bed, and it was more comfy than her little white canopy set. We had an open mother-daughter relationship. Really, I enjoyed the warmth and proximity. Though she was growing up, she was still my little girl. It did my heart good to know she was beside me, and we'd talk until we'd fall asleep. We talked about some of everything under the sun. She'd even ask what I was wearing to work the next day.

When she'd seen what I was wearing, she'd find the same color nail polish to paint my toenails and fingernails. This was one of her little rituals before dozing off. There were times I looked at this as our little campout time. But it was more of an inside camp than out. Anyhow, there are many cultures where the family sleeps together as one big happy bunch.

When she wasn't using her room for sleeping, it was a getaway for quiet time; she used it to play her music and get dressed. Once she closed those doors, the boom-box speakers blasted the sounds of Michael Jackson bouncing from wall to wall. She loved her some Michael Jackson. Her walls were plastered with his posters.

At fifteen, China learned to drive a stick-shift car. The car she used to gain experience was my 1982 silver Toyota Celica ST-Coupe convertible. I took her into a parking lot for the lessons. She learned quickly—it wasn't long before she was driving like a pro. But it wasn't until she was sixteen that China was given the car as a birthday gift. Knowing how to drive a stick was another feather in her cap.

At eighteen, China was asked to her senior prom, and she graciously accepted. I didn't hesitate to go out and buy some forest-green satin fabric for her gown. I even hired a fabulous seamstress to make her gown, and it looked absolutely gorgeous when it was finished.

On the day of prom, one thing we couldn't quite master was her wig. The natural look she wanted for this occasion just wasn't right. No matter how we tried to style it, it didn't shape up. Back then, I wasn't familiar with the head-wrapping styles. Had we known, she would have gotten a beautiful matching headpiece to accessorize the gown. We just weren't aware.

When her escort arrived all decked out, she announced, "I'm not going to the prom."

Boy oh boy, this was surely a shocker for us all—especially her date. But we couldn't begin to imagine how she felt about her look.

I once discovered that she'd created a Cuddle Card. I'm not certain at what age China made this, but it brought a smile to my face and may bring one to yours. The words she wrote can be found on the next page.

All of these defining moments give a snapshot of how quickly children develop through the cycle of life.

How many of us can readily reel off our child's snapshot moments from their tender years? Stop now and think about the question: "During those precious years, what was your child's snapshot like?"

From the maternal to the paternal grandparents, extended families mean so much to our children during their tender years. Every child should get a chance to know and receive the love of his or her paternal grandparents. When this happens, they're the lucky ones! But China wasn't so lucky, 'cause she didn't. In many ways, Craig could have pulled her into his circle, yet he'd chosen to cast her aside. He never took her around his kinfolk.

If I was asked if this hurt, I'd reply, "What do you think?"

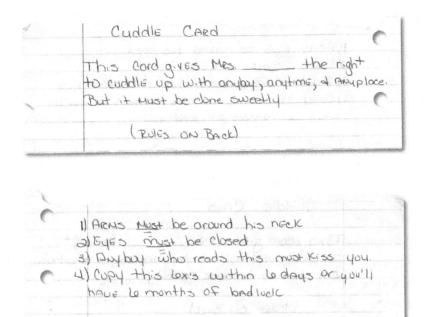

China's actual handwriting

Surely, being loved by both grandparents meant a lot to China. She was an innocent child.

We all have to make choices in life—to find relationships with soul mates, love, happiness, a place to belong, comfort, peace of mind, or whatever. And it's the choices we've made that give us gratification.

Returning to the opposite sex, emotionally, I wasn't ready for a romantic connection.

I was content with my present lifestyle. However, Peaches felt differently. Once I met Linc's friend Greg, I knew our relationship would be a casual one. Greg often came by Peaches' house for weekly card games. He stood extremely tall, like an athlete. He was dark-skinned, with a broad chest and very muscular legs. What truly impressed me was his flair for fashion. So what direction would we explore? The relationship would be a friendship. My wounds from the past were still open.

Although Greg was a unique fellow, he wasn't like the others, only looking for a night of pleasure. I enjoyed his company, particularly since he was a pure gentleman. China was fond of him, and he seemed to like her. He had a way with children, but he had none of his own. With our relationship, we stayed connected three months. But we both parted on a mellow note.

My health was on a downward spiral. Breathing had become difficult. I experienced shortness of breath and nagging chest pains with strong heartbeats. The pain was like a pressure around my chest. The symptoms had been lingering for some time. Finally, I'd gone to see a doctor and had an electrocardiogram test with other examinations. The results weren't good.

"The tests indicated an atrial septal defect and heart murmur," the doctor said. "I want you to see a cardiologist."

After hearing that news, I was nervous and frightened. I had a cardiac exam and stress test. I didn't take the results lightly when I was told, "I recommend you have surgery. If not, you'll probably be disabled by age forty."

Tears rolled down my cheeks. This was a life-threatening change. I was anxious and devastated about the surgery, and wondered about my scarred body afterwards. But most of all, I thought about the relationship I'd taken on as father and mother for China; without me, she'd have no one. The scars on my chest would just have to follow me through life. It was a major decision, but there was no question I'd have the surgery. The journey had to be approached with a positive mindset to achieve long-term success.

By June 1986, the surgery had been completed and was successful. I'd spent six weeks in the hospital recuperating from open-heart surgery. But beyond the road to recovery lay a mound of challenges.

That had been a hell of a surgery! The aftershocks felt like a concrete building had collapsed on my chest. The pain had intensified, and only doses of morphine could relieve it. If I had to rate the pain on a scale of one to ten, it rated a ten. That's how terrible it was.

Surgery was only half the battle; there were also therapeutic sessions. In particular, a chest exercise I had to do one to five times daily (which slowly increased in number). The slow movements went like this:

- Raise the arms to a height just before feeling pain.

- Bend the elbows while bringing them into the chest.
- Straighten the elbows and return them back to the sides.
- Repeat the same process.

Incredibly, vitamin D from the sun's rays had been a powerful healer. I lay outside in the backyard exposing at least forty percent of my skin, letting the sun's rays beam directly on my chest where the incisions had been made, for at least forty-five minutes to an hour daily. Amazingly, the end results meant I didn't have any keloid scars!

The next four months were filled with rounds of physical therapy sessions. Since it was now my turn to be nurtured, China showered me with care and love. Our roles had been reversed. China had advanced into adulthood, and I had drifted back into childhood. She'd even done an awesome job shopping for groceries and dealing with the finances.

I've not forgotten one special person, Kitty. Cousin Kitty was five foot six and light complected, with beautiful brown eyes and an extremely well-shaped figure. I looked forward to her visits. Each visit was always accompanied by five or six bags of groceries. The cupboards consistently overflowed, floor to ceiling, with enough food for an army. The bags stood one on top of the other, waiting to be emptied.

By November 1986, it was time to go back to work, but readapting was rather difficult. Despite this, it was my high standard of performance that got me promoted—this time into management. The new position was fast-paced. It didn't take long to fall back into the everyday routine of working and spending time with China. During this time, I felt no desire to be intimate. I was ashamed of the twelve-inch scar down my chest. Who knows, maybe that's why I suppressed those womanly desires. And the time came to face reality: China was developing into a woman—the years I feared the most. Although we spent quality time together, our lives were changing. With the shoe prints already made, we were still far from reaching the end of our journey.

The Insight

Our children are rewarding. Here are some precious gifts we can give back to them:

- Daily, tell or write them how much they are loved.
- Spend quality time eating together.
- Introduce them to educational experiences.
- Plan family outings.
- Help with schoolwork.
- Set a good example.
- Show satisfaction in what they do.

CHAPTER EIGHT

Life after Divorce

Yippee, yahoo, I'd gotten my divorce—and what a battle! Our no contest divorce was granted.

I'd gotten sick and tired of Mike going to court asking for continuation after continuation. It just went on and on, fighting over that darn property. It was crazy and foolish. What sense did it make when there was little to no equity anyway! The last time we went to court, not only did I shock his lawyer, but everyone else as well.

"Your Honor, I'd like to change my request. I don't want the property. I just want to be granted my maiden name. And that he doesn't get any of my work benefits," I told the judge.

"You're entitled to the property. Are you sure that's all you want?" she replied, wide-eyed.

"Yes, Your Honor," I firmly told her.

Everyone's faces expressed amazement and total disbelief that I wanted so little—but it was finally over. Mike got the house and all the bills. Me—I was awarded the return of my maiden name, and he wouldn't get any of my work benefits. We both couldn't have been happier. Eventually, I found out we weren't the only happy ones. When boxing up our wedding pictures, I ran across one that showed Mike and China posing together.

China had written on the back, "Don't pay any attention to the person standing next to me. My mother divorced him. I'm so happy."

That message brought the biggest smile to my face. It's amazing the things our children will do and say! A few years later (through the grapevine), I heard Mike had had money problems in keeping the house and was on the verge of losing it. There was some truth to the buzz, 'cause the house went into foreclosure. He moved down south, and that's where he met his maker. Poor soul, may he rest in peace!

China was a sophomore in high school. She had a diverse group of friends, but she still kept her high standards for education. That's why I could not refuse her wanting to have a social life. My sisters, Dana and Lyndia, felt I kept a tight choke on China—of course, I disagreed. What mother doesn't want to give their child the best life has to offer and a positive environment?

Many of China's friends were not reared in the same environment. Who knows, maybe their parents did not care to take time to get involved. Whatever the reason, it didn't affect China. She was still an easy person to befriend. She strived for everyone's love. Often, she came home troubled by cruel treatment shown by her schoolmates. Uncaring treatment is common among school kids. China could not understand why, but learned through coping. Eventually she discovered that high school was in no way the same as grammar school.

Each day, I listened to China and her girlfriends talk about the guys they found appealing. After overhearing their conversations, I knew China was no longer a child. She was maturing into a young adult. As a parent, I could not bear to cut those apron strings. There was one instance in particular that I remember.

As we watched television, she talked about attending the school dance. She had a rough time convincing me how mature she was at age fifteen. Her maturity wasn't the issue; it was her needing to be accepted by her peers. As far as dating was concerned, this wouldn't start until she was eighteen; otherwise, I'd tag along.

After our talk, China knew it was useless to try to sway me. She realized our dating ground rules implied a threesome: me, her, and her date. So she settled for telephone conversations with the boys.

China and her best friend Sheila shared a sisterly bond, one that healthy relationships are made of. Many of the girls their age were parents already;

Shelia was the exception, and she became a part of our lives, and they became inseparable.

After the divorce, my life dragged from day to day. I was not emotionally attached to anyone, and I didn't look to become romantically involved. A friendly relationship had been the extent. Although I'd befriended Wilson Burton, he expected more. In my mindset, our friendship wouldn't get any deeper. I hadn't been into him like that. Wilson was someone I'd seen around at work. He'd always seemed polite and caring about others. Sure, he had decent traits, but we were just friends. This had been what I'd hoped to achieve with Wilson—a 100 percent platonic relationship. Even so, I'd liked the fact he found me appealing; I had needed to feel wanted since the divorce.

Wilson was twice my age and divorced. At least, that's what he'd attested. The crinkled up paper he pulled from his pocket and slipped into my hand contained his cell and home phone numbers. He was average height, with a thick, trimmed, black mustache. He had a round face and wore brown, square-framed eyeglasses. When he finally approached me, I made it clear that we'd remain nothing more than friends. He had a speech impediment— he was a stutterer. Of course, when he'd strutted up in his brown and grey checkered jacket accented with that brown, wide-collared shirt, his whole outfit gave me a quick flashback: *been there, done that.* Remember, I'd once married a man who wore a similar getup.

The more we talked, I discovered Wilson was a chronic and habitual liar, a trait I despised. Definitely, his quality level dropped tremendously. China played a role in busting him out. As a parent, I'd learned to listen to a loved one's insight.

In February 1987, Wilson was still hanging around. He'd tried hard to make our relationship more than just friends. But he had become a thorn in our side. He wanted more than I cared to offer. When Wilson interacted with China, he'd shown his true colors. He'd pretended to like her, but that was fake. Frankly, I couldn't get my head around it, but it was the way he treated her, with that *you care, yet you really don't care* attitude.

"Ch–China . . . I–I'll let you drive my c–car," he said, stuttering each word.

"For real, you'd do that for me?" China eagerly responded.

With a smile, he turned back to her and said, "Su–Sure, anytime you'd like."

At one point, he'd gotten snappy in his responses. At least, that's what China told me when she asked him again outside my presence. Surely, that wasn't going to fly! I vowed to make this a pleasurable year. There I'd go on that mission thang again. But this time, I'd given myself two missions. Mission one was that China would have her sweet sixteen party—an idea she cherished. For three weeks, China and Sheila dived into making her big plans a reality.

Finally, the day arrived when our house was packed with tons of boys! Sure, a few girls were invited. Several of the boys had a spark for China. With her party going on, we had our own card game upstairs keeping us adults amused. But her little party was sho'nuff rocking. We could hear those Michael Jackson records playing loud and clear. The music bounced off the walls. They were having a grand ole time "bringing down the house," as Steve Martin and Queen Latifah would say. This was one party that wouldn't end early. Each time Peaches and I went downstairs, China was having a ball. Wow, what a party—it had gone till nearly 2 a.m.! That night would be another memorable and everlasting one for her.

Since mission one had been completed, it was time to get geared up. For the next relationship, mission two the biggest of all! And Wilson wasn't going to move on easily. All the time he'd hung around, I'd never called his house. So I made my first call when it happened—she answered!

"Hello, I'm a friend of Wilson's. Can I speak with him, please?" I'd responded.

She spoke in a low-pitched tone and said, "Sure, just a minute."

She then yelled out, "Wilson, it's your call!"

When he answered, he was stunned to hear it was me. Too bad he couldn't see the smile on my face.

With frustration, he stammered, "Hi, I–I–I was just getting ready to call you. E–Everything okay? C–Can we meet to talk about it?"

His stuttering was so rough—he probably was shaking in his boots. He'd been busted flat out. Really, we had nothing more to talk about. My calling him was just a move to stack the deck, but it unfolded a winning hand. It was even better finding out they were still together. And even if she was not his wife, it was still a woman who answered.

I'll say it again: "Been there, done that."

Lying friends were the last thing I needed. I'd proved he wasn't honest. It was difficult for him to adapt to the fact that the pussycat he once knew was a clawing, roaring tiger. Wilson tried every possible way to stay close to our lives. He tried to reconnect in some way or another, but it was a little late for that. I really had to stand fast on this, vowing to end any relationship. Wilson wasn't happy about moving on. But what choice did he have? We'd left Wilson with an imprint of our shoe print as we continued on our journey. And that relationship was history.

The Insight

It is one thing not to realize the relationship is toxic, but to know it's poisonous and stay is only asking for heartbreak. There are ways to respond and avoid toxicity:

- Untie the bonds and leave outright.
- Fill the void with healthy activities.
- Note the warning signs and red flags.
- Consider all the work involved.
- Love yourself first and foremost.
- Avoid taking to heart what is spoken.
- Listen to your instincts.

CHAPTER NINE

Letting Go to Grow Up

With less than two months before the end of school, China was excited about her summer plans. This summer she wanted to work and make extra money. I enjoyed that idea. The only problem was coping with her being a live-in babysitter. While staying at Round Lake Beach, China had gotten a paying job. She was sitting for Cousin Mark's two children, Melvin (then five years old) and Melinda (three years old), at his army-based home. For the entire summer, this would be China's home away from home. She'd reside temporarily at Fort Sheridan Army Base, where Mark was stationed.

It was China's turn to explore, take risks, and find her identity. I'd seen how she had grown. She'd become such a sweet, independent, and ingenious person. Although I was happy and proud of her accomplishments, inside there was a sad, empty feeling. This was the first summer we'd ever been apart. I loved and missed her completely. I couldn't have missed her more if she'd gone away to college. Through the sniffles, I felt such grief, as if I'd lost her for good. That's how deeply it hurt to let her go. I hadn't known if it was love or nerves.

The first week without China had been difficult. I dreaded each waking moment of those lonely summer days, hungering for a companion and a bit of conversation. To fill the emptiness, China had shown her love by calling regularly. From afar, we'd talk about the days that separated us. China had imagined her summer villa crowded with boys. But she'd found herself in a world that offered a summer of childcare memories. She'd made a commitment to babysit, so there was no dropping out. She stayed until the end, but China started to experience headaches.

When she called, sadness surfaced, and her voice echoed with pain.

"Mom, I have the most awful headache," she'd said in her soft voice.

"Baby, take a couple of aspirins, put the kids to bed, and lie down, get a nap in," I replied.

Each time she'd call, she'd mention the headaches. We'd attributed her condition to the sun—there were some scorching days during that summer of 1987. Lot of times the temperature was 97 degrees or higher.

It had become a challenge for her to overcome those headaches. China was paid big bucks for her services, but didn't want to do it again.

It's time again to step back and reflect on another moment of epiphany.

Thinking back, could the headaches have been a warning sign? Perhaps it wasn't the heat wave, but something much greater—a warning sign that her body was plagued with foreign invaders, maybe? Many times, the sign goes out of kilter. But missing the first sign of those tormenting headaches—having them go untreated—is one of my life's most regrettable and unforgettable actions. It's the thought that every parent may fear, but never wants to admit: that they've possibly been neglectful by not catching it early on. Parents, don't make that same mistake—you must take heed!

Our lives moved forward speedily. China didn't waste any time starting her shopping spree. With school starting, she planned to enter her junior year fashionably dressed. The two of us spent our quality time together in the evenings. My eyes widened listening to China talk about her day.

"Mommy, it's okay to kiss a boy as long as nothing else happens. I'm not going any further with a boy than that. I want to have a career. Becoming a lawyer takes time, and I have to stay focused," she once told me. "With my law degree, I'm going to defend underprivileged children."

As she uttered those words, I knew she no longer spoke like a child but a woman with knowledge of life.

Within a year, China would start paving her own journey. Setting her standards high, she was determined to have an education. For her, family life would come later. Yep, I was proud of her values. She would soon spread her wings. For me, two questions were unanswered: Firstly, how long would

I continue to stay in the little gray-and-white house without her? Secondly, how long would I resist her academic choices when each appeared farther than the last? Torn between fulfilling my choices or China's, I gave in to being without her. Not wanting to lose her, I accepted that she'd live on campus.

"Mommy, it's where I'll find independence and opportunity. It will be a place that offers me a sense of freedom and opportunity to achieve my personal goals," she told me.

With such a direct statement, how could anyone reject their child's wishes? Yeah, it's hard to cut those apron strings. But, it was time—time to let go and watch her grow up. During the final months, China remained at the top of her class. She believed that hard work, dedication, and determination were the key. Our time was precious as the clock wound down. We cherished our quality time. Nothing could separate us from those moments, nothing at all—or so I thought.

Suddenly, the road beyond had no slopes, circles, hills, valleys, or mountains. There in the distance was a broken thorn—a thorn that meant *separation*. Even though we had a relationship strong enough to survive any cracks, it was the last thing we needed. Then again, separation wasn't the worst thing—or was it? The shoe prints we made next changed our journey's path forever. And it made our relationship stronger.

The Insight

Listening is an important aspect of parenting, and it helps us to become aware of our children's needs.

- Listen carefully to your children. Over time, it will make a difference.
- Listening is one of the most valuable tools.
- The teen years are usually the most challenging when it comes to communicating with children.
- Don't make the mistake of not listening to their needs—tune in.
- Their speech sends out signals—take heed.

CHAPTER TEN

The Diagnosis—*Cancer Strikes*

I changed jobs in August of 1987 because of the surgery. The place where I had my chest split wide open was Saint James Hospital in Blue Island. Even though my recovery was going well, I chose to shift jobs. I started to work on the retail side, which required sharpening my finance skills. To broaden my knowledge, I was sent to our training academy in Washington. While I was there, China stayed with Dana for two weeks. My niece Sara and China loved being with each other. Although they had their differences, there were more pleasurable moments than anything else.

The first week at the academy was good, between training classes and viewing sites. But it wasn't the same back home.

Dana called and said, "She has taken down sick. I tried a few home remedies, now we're going to Ingalls Hospital. What's your insurance information?"

"Okay, we got the Blue Cross Blue Shield Family Plan. Here's the fed ID number, and here is our group number," I told her.

"Don't worry. We'll call you once we get back," she replied.

As it happened, China and Sara had had one of their foolish, girly fall-outs. Then China had fallen to the ground and complained of backaches. But it was the next call that sent me into a tizzy.

China's normally soft-spoken, whispery voice cried out, "Mommy, he took some X-rays and sent me home before the X-rays came back. But he thinks it's just muscle spasms and told me to go home and soak in a tub of hot water. Mommy, it still hurts."

With that said, I took the next flight home.

China tried the hot water treatments, even using Epsom salts to break down the inflammation and pain. Still, the home remedies just weren't easing her aching back. She tossed and turned, struggling to sleep. Her body was as contorted as that of the hunchback of Notre Dame. She paced throughout the night, moving slowly from one end of the room to the other. I believed her pain and suffering were more than simple muscle spasms. It was early morning when we arrived at my doctor's office. Didn't take much for Dr. Kumar to give China the once over. His anger escalated when we told him the staff at Ingalls Hospital had let her leave in such a condition, without waiting for the results.

"We must get her back to the hospital! She can barely walk!" he yelled in an outraged tone.

"And it won't be that darn Ingalls Hospital," I interjected.

This time she'd go to South Suburban Hospital in Hazel Crest. For five days, she was probed and prodded as he reviewed test after test and consulted with doctor after doctor. It took a staff of six physicians. Each one required more information than the last to make a diagnosis. The questions they asked would've made any mother uneasy: Had she ever had intercourse? Were there any noticeable changes in her body? Were there any signs of tiredness or weight loss? How was her appetite? Did she complain of fevers or night sweats?

I probed them, "Why are you asking me all this?"

Her illness was easier shown than explained. Perhaps that's why they took me to China's bedside and placed my hand on her abdomen and under her armpits. They felt as hard as bricks. Afterward, the doctor took my hand and pressed it against the side of her neck; there, too, was another growth.

A diseased relationship can be a mind-blowing creature. The weight it lays on the mind is torturous. With my eyes cast upward as my teeth clenched down on my lower lip, I thought, *Are these abnormalities real? If so, why are they lurking inside? What does it all mean? Why has God chosen us to walk this journey?*

"We are going to run some tests. We won't know anything for at least three days. You'll just have to be patient with us. She's in good hands now," one doctor said.

Dr. Jose, a medical oncologist, performed a fine-needle aspiration on her to remove fluids and take samples of her spleen. We waited for the results to be read by a pathologist. Facing the unknown was a journey no one should endure alone. Time rapidly passed as the doctors were preparing to share their prognosis. And word of China being ill spread like wildfire through the family grapevine.

It wasn't long before members of Craig's family came to the hospital. I was happy to see his sisters, Julia and Netti. Julia had always shared a special place in China's heart. Once Julia entered the room bearing down on her crutch, alongside Netti, China's face lit up with joy. This was the first sign of happiness since she entered the hospital. Out of all three of his sisters, Julia was the one who always showed concern. I hadn't really seen Netti in a while. We both knew there would be plenty of time for chit-chat. The two of them needed to spend time comforting China. Their love and support would give us the strength to overcome the rocky road ahead.

Finally we met with the doctors. The look on their faces said it all.

Dr. Jose delivered the horrid news. "Your daughter has cancer."

Those are words no parent should ever have to hear and bear. It was devastating. The tumor in her ovary was benign, but in other parts it was malignant: Hodgkin disease. She needed surgery to remove one of her ovaries. Dr. Jose stood in front of us with his sparkling blue eyes, curly brown hair, pointed nose, tanned complexion, and slim physique. He was a straightforward person all the way.

"The cancer formed in China's lymph nodes is already at stage four. Her treatment process will begin with chemotherapy because it exists in more than one area. Although there's no cure for this disease, its survival rate after treatment is relatively high," he told us.

During our consultation, we learned a lot about cancer relationships and this particular disease, Hodgkin lymphoma. In other words, it became an educational lesson in the field of cancer: the stages, various approaches on how to tackle it, and the many side effects.

The next four weeks, Julia and Netti stayed close by, comforting us every step of the way. They, too, felt this heavy burden. Their presence and support was like sisterly love. Now, with all my four sisters—Dana, Lyndia, Julia, and Netti—surrounding us, there was no mountain we couldn't climb. Each day China remained hospitalized, we were there encouraging her to focus on a full recovery. It was best that she not know the seriousness of her illness. The hardest task was to make certain her doctors and nurses wouldn't reveal the news. We all vowed that I would be the one to tell her. Each visit grew more complex. We waited patiently as the time approached for the first major surgery. She learned less than the truth about why her ovary needed to come out and about those experimental drugs that would attack the disease.

The wait seemed endless as another doctor, Dr. Hacker, examined China for the surgery.

As we stood in the corridor, Dr. Hacker reappeared with her eyebrows raised, eyes wide, and mouth hung open. She hesitated before speaking.

"I can't give her a Pap smear. She's still a virgin," she finally said.

I believe I even saw Dr. Hacker shedding a tear or two. As the tears ran down our faces, we knew China deserved better than what life was offering. There she was, a child who hadn't begun to experience life nor become exposed to real womanhood. Still she'd have to struggle to gain a winning hand. Dr. Hacker decided to go ahead with the surgery, vowing to remove both ovaries only if necessary. While the surgery lingered on, I paced back and forth, drinking coffee after coffee. Each time a surgeon came in the waiting room, I feared their presence, wondering if China had made it through. Watching the clock tick slowly, I watched Dr. Hacker working to pull China through. With sweat rolling down her brow and face, there stood the lady in her white jacket. She bore an even darker skin complexion with her thick blackish-brown hair pulled back in a bun style. Once I rose, she brushed her left hand across her forehead to wipe the sweat from her brow.

"Good news, the surgery was a success. She has pulled through just fine. I only had to remove one ovary. She still has one for her childbearing years. We're moving her to the recovery room now, and you can go back to see her."

As I looked down at China's helpless body, I could see her innocence.

It gave me a feeling of pride to know her body was untouched. Wow, she was still a virgin! My daughter of sixteen years had chosen not to explore those womanly desires. Perhaps it was the guidance she respected with the nurturing of a mother's love.

When China awoke, she cracked a slight smile and said, "Hi Mommy." We exchanged smiles of love and hope.

"Water, water!" she murmured from a drug-induced state. Her eyes barely opened as I brought water to her lips.

I was devastated when China said, "Mommy, I had those lumps for a while. I was waiting until I graduated to tell you. Did they remove them?"

"Yes," I replied, tearing up.

There's nothing like a mother's passion to see her child succeed. Although I respected her drive, I had difficulty embracing her reasoning. In her youth, I'd always honored her privacy. Rightfully so—it was the thing to do. If I had observed her body in the flesh, the relationship with foreign invaders could've been detected and caught early on. In any case, it's what we parents need to consider—seeking opportunities to attack a diseased relationship in its early stages.

Over the next couple of weeks, China remained at the hospital. It was Dr. Jose's intention for her to receive an initial dose of chemotherapy while there. This would allow the staff to monitor her reactions. She experienced no difficulties as her small, fragile body took the doses of chemotherapy. Dr. Jose was confident the treatment would work, and she'd continue with the doses as an outpatient.

After China was released, every Friday she'd return to the medical center at Intermed Oncology Associates in Homewood. Her blood was drawn weekly; biweekly, she'd receive meds. For China's sake, it was agreed that we would refer to chemo only as medicine, which we'd call the meds. Once we arrived and met the staff, our relationship became a pleasant one. The head oncology nurse, LaTris, greeted us with open arms, which made us feel welcome. She was a petite person who didn't wear more than a size 5 in her white nurse's uniform. She had the most beautiful deep tan for her Caucasian complexion. Her hair was light blonde with the cutest short cut. As LaTris explained the pros and cons of the medication, I watched China's nose wrinkle and her lips hang loose. For the first time, she showed her emotions. Perhaps it was the side effects that triggered her look of disgust:

- Appetite and fertility loss
- Hair loss or thinning
- Nausea
- Constipation
- Facial acne
- A sore mouth
- Skin and mouth dryness
- Feeling tired and run down (a result of low red blood cells)
- Low resistance to infections (due to low white blood cells)
- Bruising or bleeding easily (if platelet counts run low)

Her chances of producing children were minimal, as a result of the treatment and the removal of one of her ovaries. The use of chemo drugs could cause sterilization. And its effects stopped her menstrual cycle.

We had another hard blow later on; we were all shocked to learn Julia had been diagnosed with breast cancer. Unlike China, her disease was identified in its earliest stage. Having regular physical checkups and doing her breast self-exams made a good prognosis possible. Fortunately, there wasn't a need for breast removal or even reconstruction. Julia's care only required treatment. Surprisingly, she and China had the same oncologist. Now Julia needed love, comfort, and support. This meant her shoe prints on our journey would come to an end. It was her turn to focus on a full recovery and battle the relationship with her disease.

Julia's fight was long and hard, but she won the war. She was one of many survivors who have contributed to the high rate of survival. As a hard-working amputee, she owns and manages a very lucrative business and lives a fruitful, cancer-free life in a suburban city about twenty miles outside Chicago.

Here's where Julia's imprint ended. Not only had Julia left our presence, but Netti pulled out as well.

There was no time for hard feelings with Netti's departure. So, as we began a new journey, our shoe prints must walk alone alongside this diseased relationship.

The Insight

Having a diseased relationship is hard enough for an adult to digest; God forbid you hear the words "Your child has cancer."

- It brings a crippling effect that touches all members of the family.
- It becomes an emotional challenge to tell a child.
- For an adult, its emotional impact is devastating. Imagine the degree when it's a child.
- No person is ever ready to know he or she has cancer—let alone a child.

CHAPTER ELEVEN

Spreading Rumors

China's eagerness to attend school was overwhelming; she was excited about becoming a senior. Despite her illness, she met her class assignments. The pain pierced deeper when her hair started shedding. As each strand thinned and faded away, I convinced China to wear a wig. Each morning as I combed her wig, it took a lot of strength to hold my tears back. Watching the tears running down her cheeks broke my heart.

The first two weeks of school went well. China would come home happy from being with her classmates. But it didn't last long! When the call came in that day, I could barely understand her through her sobs and whimpers. "Mommy, I left school. I ain't going back, either."

This was something Peaches and I feared would happen one day. So I called Peaches to meet us at home and left in a panic. Rushing home, there were many thoughts drifting through my mind.

Where would we go from here? What happened to provoke her actions? Hadn't China suffered enough? What injustice had the school put on her?

By now, the whites of my eyes were bulging. The closer I'd got to home, the more fearful I became.

Both of us arrived around the same time. We'd barely entered the kitchen when we saw China bawling her eyes out. Through her sobs and anger, we found out that China had left because of cruel and unjust treatment from her peers. She'd always been gullible and naïve, and she yearned for acceptance.

At the lunch table in the cafeteria, several of her classmates had gotten up and left. They all moved to another table, and their actions crushed her. It was Sheila who told her why. Rumors had spread that she was suffering from AIDS, leukemia, herpes, or some other hideous toxic disease. This news was shocking and sent her into an isolated state. It broke her little heart. No matter how I fixed her wig to make it look natural, it only gave the impression that she was contagiously diseased.

So I spent the next two hours explaining how cruel society could be, especially her generation. When ending, this is what I said: "Understanding one's illness begins with parental upbringing. We parents do not have answers for those who have been chosen to endure such a horrifying fate. Yet, those who suffer, God has chosen for reasons unbeknownst to any human—you are a special one. Through Him, you're blessed with the inheritance of courage and strength to help conquer your battles. We don't know why people do what they do—we only know it's done. So you must use your inheritance to do His will."

My words of wisdom sunk into her heart and mind. Understanding surfaced on her face as she nodded up and down with a smile. We managed to convince China to return to school. Her school days weren't happy ones, but Sheila was always there to lift her spirits. Although China found her school unpleasant, she dreaded Fridays even more. For us, Fridays meant treatment days. According to her, the treatments felt like her stomach lining was being ripped apart. Obviously, she started experiencing many of the side effects: nausea and vomiting, fatigue, dry skin, and appetite loss. Her healthy tissues were now toxic body parts.

Since China became ill, my life was centered on her. I had no time to share with others. But Cousin Kitty felt differently. She was always willing to lift my spirits no matter what. So when Dr. Jose assured China she could attend college if her condition improved, Kitty was ready to play Cupid. She and her companion, Frank, had been together two years. Frank was a much older man—about twice her age. He was short, wore thick, round-framed glasses, and had mingled gray and black hair. There wasn't anything he wouldn't give her. Kitty wanted this to be true for the man of my dreams. At this time, dreams were all I wanted. But in my heart, I knew Kitty meant well.

When she arranged to hook me up with a blind date, she wasn't stopping short: she set the stage with dimmed lights. Sitting on the couch was this strange-looking man—I could see him without straining. He was a tall, fair-skinned man with a hungry grin, who was stacked with broad shoulders. He bore an even more noticeable feature: a head the size of a watermelon! I could not imagine ever seeing such a melon head. Surprisingly, there it was and belonged to the man they called Steven London. Steven was Frank's cousin, and he was expected to become the center of my life. Frankly, he wasn't pleasing to the eye, appeared to be about sixty-two years old, and wore bifocal glasses. Really, I don't know why I bothered to stay, but I hung around. Somehow, I found myself attracted to older men. They became more like father figures. Perhaps I still longed for the affection of my dad. Yeah, he was wrong for what he'd done, but he was still my daddy, and I missed him deeply.

Shortly after I arrived at Kitty's place, the food was ready. Kitty served cocktails and hors d'oeuvres for starters. Our main course was a salad, filet mignon smothered in mushrooms and dark brown gravy, mashed potatoes, Brussels sprouts, and hot, soft, buttery rolls, along with a mellow Merlot wine. For dessert, she served lemon cream pie. Wow, what a delicious meal— it was worth staying!

Drifting back to earth, I looked around to see the biggest wildcat grin on his face. The way things were going, we made the best of the evening. I knew nothing of Steven. Even though there were some negative vibes in the air, I'd always spoken against forming negative opinions—best to acquaint oneself with the person.

"Tell me something about yourself?" I asked Steven.

He made sure to tell me, "I own a three-flat building and my aunt lives with me. The building is over on 83rd and Champlain. I worked as a machinist at a factory. I'm retired now and losing sight in one of my eyes— it's the left one. I'm not married anymore, but I have two sons. My oldest son is thirty-five, and the youngest is thirty-one."

Boy, Steven was a running faucet with the gift of gab. He surely wasn't one to pass over a conversation. I made the mistake of giving a nonverbal gesture of being pleased. He babbled on and on. Sadly, he even revealed the story of how he lost two fingers. "You see, my fingers were crushed in one of those machines," he said, as he wiggled his finger nubs in front of me.

This guy had endured one trauma after another. Still, I'd enjoyed hearing his sorrows. It was as though our diseased relationship had vanished. As we welcomed each other, the evening stretched into morning. For the next few weeks, we covered many topics. Our lives appeared similar. The newness of our acquaintance buried any blockage to developing a commitment. Steven's presence would be a new imprint on our journey.

The Insight

No child should have to endure bullying, harassment, or teasing. The toxicity of these actions can cause long-term relationship problems. There are many reasons why kids are cruel:

- Lack of love and attention.
- Lack of education about the effects of bullying or one's illness.
- Improper upbringing.
- To boost popularity among peers.
- As a cry for help.
- Just plain ignorance.

CHAPTER TWELVE

Treatment Dazes

By now, the symptoms of her cancer relationship were clearly noticeable. China weighed less than one hundred pounds and still needed treatment. Every Friday came like clockwork. When she wasn't getting treatments, she'd have her blood drawn and tested. Her cell counts and platelets had to remain normal. When her counts dropped, she couldn't get any treatments. Many times, the complete blood count workup showed her platelets were low. But her other cell counts or blood chemistry tests stayed stable. Whenever her platelets were low, she'd have a platelet transfusion and no treatments. There were periods when she was hospitalized.

Treatment plans are designed for each patient. Our particular program involved injections twice a month with weekly visits to the doctor. Her tiny veins took in the mixture of chemo fluids. I felt the warmth of her small hand as she reached to gain strength from mine. If I recall correctly, the first round of chemotherapy included ABVD agents; these were all changed later on. All agents were given intravenously. She had baby veins that tended to jump or collapse when poked with a needle. LaTris had to pump up a good vein before prepping the skin area and inserting a fine needle into the vein. She prepared the area with a see-through dressing for protection. The medication dripped at a slow, continuous rate, allowing absorption into her bloodstream.

China would groan as tears rushed down her cheeks. Without us saying anything, our eyes would connect. We dreaded those scheduled Fridays. Each injection brought us closer to the end of treatment, but that wasn't until next March—way off, since it was still just the month of December.

Christmas wouldn't be the same. The traditional love and cheerfulness was missing, replaced by love and sadness. China's sickness dampened our spirits. The severity of her sickness had stricken the hearts of us all. Openly, we'd speak about other everyday crises, but this topic wouldn't be talked about. Our circuit of silence would remain medically sealed, for now. The time must be right to reveal how ill China really was; somehow, the time never seemed right. She was delicate and sensitive, but she had to learn the truth someday. Until then, all she'd know was that her illness required doses of medicine. China always had a way of expressing her disappointment. Her thoughts and questions glistened from her eyes. China was gifted with eyes that made a statement without words, a trait she used to her advantage. She had those dreamy eyes that would make one fall in love. She was contained in thought, but her eyes lifted up to me. It was a look that appeared to say, *Why me? I haven't begun to live! I must take control of this thing inside me.*

Even though those words weren't spoken, her eyes said them. For the next two weeks, China moped about as if the world had crumbled beneath her feet—a sign of depression. This was just the initial phase, and since depression is one of the symptoms of cancer, I wasn't so alarmed.

China knew very little of my association with Steven, and best it stayed that way. During the holidays, we continued to keep our weekly appointments. It didn't take her long to adapt to treatments provided by her two favorite nurses, LaTris and Joyce. When LaTris wasn't giving the treatments, Joyce stepped in. Joyce, too, had a special knack for making the sick feel well. Again, it's the way they nurtured their patients and how gently they administered their treatments.

From the sidelines, it was painful watching China take in the toxic fluids that were seeping through those tubes and passing into her veins. Her tiny veins collapsed even when the blood was drawn. It got to the point where she needed a central venous catheter inserted. The tube was implanted in her upper body, near her breast, and required routine maintenance, but it provided easy access to her veins. Staff members were able to draw blood and give injections from the tubing insertion. China would gag as she regurgitated into a small container placed beside her chair. No question she had strength unknown to many humans, and at such a young age. Her treatments lasted approximately one and a half to two hours. This variance was due to the rotation of medications and contingent on whatever doses were given.

Driving home, her side effects included weakness and drowsiness. At one point, I glanced over to see her hanging out the car window. All of her body's fluids seemed to be coming out.

After each expulsion, she'd cry out, "Oh God, help me, help me!"

With each treatment, we gained knowledge about what was to be expected. On treatment day (called "Our Meds Day"), China conditioned herself to eat less. By the time we'd arrive home, the vomiting would progress through three stages: green to yellow to clear. Whatever treatment she'd received took its toll on her. It did not take long to realize her Friday meal would be a can of chicken noodle soup or mini portions of food to help settle her stomach. She would sleep from midday till early dawn—a sign of being fatigued. But once awake, she was alert and vibrant. No one would imagine her suffering from the night before.

Her eagerness to return to school demonstrated inner strength. China could hardly wait to mingle with her classmates. And already she was making career moves, applying for one scholarship after another. She stood firm with her decision to become independent. Her next step toward self-fulfillment would be accomplished through living on campus. As a parent, I wasn't pleased with the idea. But between her and Dr. Jose, I was outnumbered—he backed her wholeheartedly. He felt this move would keep her preoccupied and continuing her struggle against the Big C.

Dr. Jose took me aside and said, "I'm really impressed that she's determined to go to school. If she concentrates on school, she's not thinking about her illness. We need to give her whatever makes her happy in life."

After completing the treatments, the criteria required quarterly follow-up visits for imaging tests. These tests would determine whether the treatments were successful. Of course, it would be contingent on the doctor which imaging test was performed: computed tomography scan, magnetic resonance imaging, or a gallium scan.

In 1989, China expected to finish her treatments, and I was waiting for the day that every parent anxiously waits for—seeing their child walk across the graduation stage and enter the cycle of adulthood. The next three months flew by rapidly. China stayed in school despite her routine visits for treatments. By March 1989, we'd finally approached the completion of her treatments, and China was filled with high spirits that lifted her morale. Her positive mood and the smile she kept on her face was truly a blessing.

There we were, waiting patiently for a clean bill of health two weeks after her last visit.

Dr. Jose told us, "China, you need to go to the hospital and take X-rays for a computed tomography scan and gallium."

We tried desperately to keep the faith, believing no other treatments were needed. The results weren't going to be known until our next visit. Keeping on with our normal activities, I showered her with love and affection. Thinking the chemo was powerful enough to operate full force, we had no idea our joy would be shattered.

We both had grown to love and admire Dr. Jose. As he entered the room, his eyes were smiling and the corners of his mouth turned up. He was always an upbeat person.

But his positive expression disappeared. Dr. Jose said, "China, we've still to find the answers. You'll need to undergo radiation treatments for another six to eight weeks."

For a moment, I had to stop and take in a deep breath. It was not only painful hearing those words, but heartbreaking to watch the tears roll down her cheeks. Even though the chemotherapy had destroyed some of the cancer cells, it didn't kill them all. Radiation would be a way to target the remaining toxic cells, aiming the rays at their precise location. During these next two months, I knew I had to be strong for both of us, especially with graduation just three months away. This was another obstacle, but I continued to hold back my tears. China would never see that side, but it wasn't easy pretending things were okay.

As a caregiver, these are the words of advice I'd give anyone: Remain strong, and never let them see you cry. But if you must, cry behind closed doors.

I knew I couldn't shed a tear in front of her. Together, we would strengthen her odds for remission.

I'd started working shorter hours since radiation was four times a week. I felt there wasn't a problem readjusting my work schedule. It could be rather easy to fade into the woodwork, since we were staffed with six supervisors in one location. Eventually, I began looking forward to spending those four hours with the customers and employees. Perhaps it was a method to camouflage my problems. Many times I wore a painted smile. Just another means of carrying the cross we were chosen to bear. I pretended everything in my life was hunky-dory. Although our castle was crumbing beneath our feet, China didn't see it that way. She was determined to pursue her dream—as a scholar of law. I was proud to have raised a daughter with such high aspirations.

Difficult as it was to face tragedy and the unknown, the pain became even deeper and harder. The baby I bore seventeen years ago was slipping from life. Through the years, she had always been full of vigor, adding a spark to everyone's life. Now she was transforming—leaving behind her beautiful smile, energy, and spirit for life. Oftentimes, her eyes held back the tears of her aches and pains. As I'd comfort her, I saw those hidden tears in her sunken, saddened eyes. Her body was frail and bony, so frail that she wore three times the clothing just to emulate thickness. If she stood sideways, she'd fade away into the background. No one could imagine the thoughts going through her mind. Whatever they were, they were working overtime on her. To stack her weight, I observed her putting on a triple layer of jeans. And this ripped out my heart. As a parent, that was a painful sight. Perhaps parents need to pay attention to their children for developmental changes that could affect their bodies, particularly in their tender years. Of course, let's not forget our own bodily changes. Should we catch these invaders early on, it could make for a positive outcome medically. Had this happened in our case, we might have beaten the odds.

China's appearance changed drastically as a result of the radiation treatments. As the rays beamed down on her darkening body, her complexion was roasting beyond recognition. No matter how I tried to satisfy China, her moods became increasingly unpredictable. Although angered by the discoloration of her skin, she was happy that her hair had begun to grow back. Some may consider this a minor issue, but for her, it was positively meaningful.

By the beginning of June, China was finishing the last round of radiation. She'd missed several treatments due to a decrease in her white cell count. China endured her treatments, but she didn't find pleasure in making preparations for graduation. She didn't want to walk across that stage wearing a wig. At times, I caught her staring at several of her old pictures, as though mesmerized by their features. The snapshots showed her with a head of black hair. As she looked at them, salty tears crept down her face.

Around the house, she wore a bandana. But not to school—that certainly would've brought attention to her illness. Now there are a variety of head coverings one can wear to be stylish that are specifically designed for patients going through cancer. Scarves, turbans, and hats are used to coordinate with outfits. If I'd known at the time, we could've taken this approach to enhance her beauty—China always had been a fashion plate. But then again, the diseased relationship was our secret.

It was June 8, 1989, and a joyous occasion. Graduation day had come. It was a memorable moment in our lives, with cheers, smiles, and laughter filling the air. Their gowns were purple and gold. The students gathered outside the building hugging and kissing each other. Peaches and I could barely hold back the tears as we watched them give their farewells. The evening ended with a night of fun and feasting for friends and family. China was on her way to a life of challenges: a struggle for survival and the desire to live on campus. The time had come to grow, accept, and respect her wishes. The imprint of our shoe prints had taken a different path; we were heading on a cancerous journey.

The Insight

All these effects have one thing in common: a relationship with cancer.

- Fatigue.
- Secondary cancer.
- Weight loss.
- Skin discoloration.
- Depression.
- Infertility.

She began disappearing before our eyes.
No matter how we tried to pretend, . . .

CHAPTER THIRTEEN

Challenges—School Dazes

China had been accepted at two colleges. One offered a high caliber of education: Northern Illinois University. The other had a reputation for teaching the students to party: Southern Illinois University. She had no problem accepting the latter. Somehow the words spoken by Dr. Jose became clearly understood.

He repeated his words again later: "We need to make sure China enjoys whatever life has to offer." Did he suspect something more, or was it just his way of giving her permission to take on new challenges? Either way, all he required of us was our routine visits. And with the disease in remission, she was permitted to go downstate, although she was expected to return in October for a follow-up.

China always knew I was scared to live alone. I was the kind of parent who needed someone to look after her. China was the real caretaker of this family. She had taken the weight of doing all the cooking.

Whenever there were cooked meals, she was the one who prepared them. She had a way of making food taste agreeable.

I knew it was not a good choice, but fast food chains and I had become the best of friends. China needed to focus on her studies and health, trusting I'd be strong enough to go it alone. But with Steven waiting in the wings, I wasn't going to be alone. With China away, Steven had started hanging out with me.

We'd gone grocery shopping together, eaten meals, gone to the movies, and visited his friends and mine. Since I wasn't much of a cook, we dined out regularly—three times a week, at least. We enjoyed being together and comforting our loneliness. I'd grown to care deeply for Steven. He was a loving, caring, supportive, and accepting person. I realized I loved him, but I wasn't in love with him. Simply put, the chemistry hadn't ignited. I loved Steven for being that wonderful man and accepting sexuality as a limited priority.

But we'd only hung out as friends a short while before he asked to live together. Yeah, he started making offers to move in.

"Why are you paying rent over here? I got that two-floor apartment, come move in with me. You don't have to pay a dime. Save your money," he'd say repeatedly.

"No, thanks," I repeatedly replied.

After a very brief period, we'd gotten along great and started hanging out more. Finally, his proposal sparked my interest. Being supported, financially and emotionally, sounded great.

Plus, I'd done some cohabitation before, and this guy deeply loved us.

China wasn't pleased with the move-in at first, but that changed when she learned that Steven planned to redo the basement—just for her. Steven felt she'd enjoy having her own space whenever there was a school break. I wasn't overwhelmed about his Aunt Ethel living in the same house, and I'd become inspired by her character and boldness. She had no qualms in standing her ground—truly, my kind of lady.

Our move-in hadn't gone as smoothly as expected. Within one day, Steven had made a mess of things. In his sneaky way, Steven thought he'd conceal our move-in from his Aunt Ethel. I was completely humiliated when Ethel arrived and found out we'd moved in.

"What's going on up in here? Tell me summin', or do I have to figure out myself?" She dragged her words out.

"Yeah, forgot to tell you, today is the day my lady and her daughter move in," Steven replied. "And the place is big enough, with room for all of us."

"That may be so, and nice if you'd told me 'fore now. I mighta wanted to move out, myself," Ethel told him.

I stood there, unable to respond. I just let them talk it through. Of course,

I understood why this hadn't set well with her. What woman wouldn't want to know who's invading her home?

It took a while, but Ethel and I managed to deal openly. We started going grocery shopping, hanging out at the malls, and socializing with some of her elderly friends. China settled into our new environment, decorating her basement apartment, where Steven had a beautiful black-and-yellow checkered floor installed, along with a separate walk-in closet. The huge closet was for the both of us, China and me. He'd even installed a private bathroom for China. She wasn't going back to school until mid-August, so she had thirty days to let the dust settle. The move had done much to boost Steven's ego: he pranced through the apartment grinning from ear to ear like a hunter on the prowl, as the contractors were busy at work.

China had no problems sharing her true feelings about Steven. No matter how he'd tried to win her love, it was meaningless. She wanted nothing from him but to be left alone. She was not happy with me either, since I'd uprooted our lives.

So the days moved very slowly as the four of us adjusted to our new lifestyle. Ethel and I fell into our roles as far as the house went.

I'd never claimed to be a Suzy Homemaker—surely cooking was not my niche. But it was a task that Ethel did well. For me, cleaning was the one thing I tackled easily. Although she tried her hand at it by giving the house the once-over, I backtracked her moves. Over it all hung the cancer, however.

There was no hope of removing those toxic invaders manifesting in China's body. She began disappearing before our eyes. No matter how we tried to pretend, she was far from recovery. China was chosen to have a continuous diseased relationship. But school had become the center of her life. It was the one thing she concentrated on. And once a month, we kept the appointments with Dr. Jose. Someday, we thought, maybe one of those monthly visits would work a miracle.

While China was at school, I tried to make the best of life. It hadn't taken long to acknowledge that Ethel and I would have to shove out an abundance of love and effort to become friends. As a parent of a child with cancer, I had my moods, and Ethel certainly had her ways. So when we butted heads, our feelings for one another turned upside down.

One time, I decided that I wanted to give a livelier touch to the apartment by slapping some paint on the walls and laying a little carpet. Guess what: Ethel took this as an insult to her housekeeping skills. After that, her temper flared horribly. Boy, oh boy, the name calling that went back and forth was quite distasteful. Steven paced the sidewalk as Ethel and I went toe to toe, willing to let us thump it out.

For his part, Steven had no problems conjuring up little lies. One time he told me Kitty had been by, but when I called her, it turned out that he had lied. It wouldn't surprise me if he enjoyed lying just to hear himself talk.

Between Ethel and Steven, it wasn't easy to tell which one was wearing my nerves thin. Each one was batting a thousand. Even so, this was a web I'd spun myself.

After the discord with Aunt Ethel, things didn't sit right with me. I'd disrespected her on her turf. It had been her domain before mine. I felt lousy and miserable about the goings-on. Still, when I went to speak to Ethel, it took the big in me to offer peace.

"We are two people with different values. Let's face it: we all have our moody and snooty ways. I'd like to make amends for my actions. I apologize for the hurt caused," I told her.

We both extended our arms and hugged. It was there that our relationship began to become richer. We learned to interact woman to woman, sip coffee together, and fix meals as one. (Well, she'd cook and I'd become the assistant.) She'd even ask about China's well-being at times.

As for the other people in our lives during this period, it wasn't always so easy.

Lord knows we could have done without the interference of Ora Bea, China's grandmother on her father's side. It was our first and only phone call from China's granny. If you think it was a pleasant one, think again. With no caller ID device, I picked up the phone after two rings. On the other end was Ora Bea. She was rude and dismissive—she didn't say hello, and she didn't ask to speak with her granddaughter or even how she was doing. She just lit right into it.

"I want to talk to you," Ora Bea said firmly. Then she yelled out, "Stop trying to take my son to court! China is eighteen and there's no reason for this. There's just no reason at all!"

That's it, I've had it, I thought. I wasn't going to allow her to talk anymore.

I interrupted, "Lady, the one you really need to be talking with is your son. Our daughter has cancer. And that's reason enough. C'mon lady, I won't listen to any more of that talk. Don't ever call us again."

The next sound Ora Bea heard was the click of a receiver. And we didn't hear from her after that.

I didn't understand how Ora Bea entangled herself in our lives all of a sudden. Did Craig run back and tell Mommy, or what?

Although it is remembered, that scene has stayed in the past. Of course, she's been forgiven. I refuse to hold onto the negative. Ora Bea's presence was an imprint molded as part of our diseased relationship.

Her detachment showed her true feelings toward China.

The Insight

Disinterested or deadbeat, see it for its worth:

- The apple doesn't fall far from the tree—like mother, like son.
- When grandparents lack interest and become deadbeats, they are heartless. These people can't be changed into something other than what they are.

Things to consider:

- Make up for the disheartened attitudes through extra love and attention.
- Nurture the child's relationship with the caring grandparent.
- Gear their attention to what they have—not what they don't have.

CHAPTER FOURTEEN

Exposing the Big "C"

By December 1989, we were heartbroken to learn the cancer had returned. This brought on shock and fear. Fear of the uncertainties, of fighting the unknown. Could this phase be the beginning of the end? Or was it really the end of a beginning? There we were, bombarded with hospitals, medical bills, needles, catheters, platelets, treatments, side effects, and a mound of aches and pains. When she found out, China drifted back into depression.

She spent the next twelve weeks undergoing chemotherapy, pumped with pints of platelets administered to keep her from bruising or bleeding easily. Life for China became a revolving door. A young dreamer whose life was struck by an archer who shot one bull's-eye after another. No school, no hair, and no lifelong dreams. Her dreams and hopes receded from the inevitable. At eighteen, China's life was again on hold, and it was time to expose the Big C.

There was no easy way to tell my child she had cancer. But she'd finally know the truth behind her illness. She'd know how much I loved her, that there was hope, and that I was there for her. Most importantly, it was time she made her own decisions in the fight to be rid of this diseased relationship.

After those long-overdue tears, China asked many questions. There was much to expose about this relationship, and to see how hard she took it all tore me apart.

Once she knew about the disease, we vowed to keep it a secret, fight back together, and go on praying and hoping. When I asked if there were any more questions, I got the most shocking response.

"Mommy, do you think God will cure me?" It was the one question she asked as her tears dripped.

"Yes, baby. When we pray, God answers all prayers," I replied.

It was all that could be said or done. I embraced her words and held her close to my bosom. From that day forth, every Sunday we went to church to pray for a miracle.

As the weeks passed, she lost a lot of weight—over 25 pounds. There was little I could do but make certain she was fed. It was imperative China kept her strength—she had no immune system to ward off infections. Each time I entered her room, my heart fluttered. There she sat in the center of the bed, gazing at her school pictures as the tears rolled down her cheeks.

China endured the phases of treatments just as she had in the past. There were times she needed platelets. Normally, this occurred when her temperature climbed to over 100 degrees. But by the spring of 1990, China recuperated from the chemo treatments. She expected to return to school in the fall after getting a clean bill of health.

My life with Steven was going nowhere. I caught him in one lie after another.

"You got a call from one of those apartment owners. They didn't have any more vacancies. But I don't remember the person's name who called," he said one night.

"What the devil are you talking about, dude? You ought to stop it. You're lying for no reason. I haven't been looking for no darn apartment. You are such a liar," I told him.

That incident drove me over the edge. Knowing he was lying, he sat there with egg on his face.

It was the last straw! With everything happening to China, my nerves were off-kilter. I was ready to move on. And it didn't take much to convince China. Despite what had occurred previously between us, Ethel said she wished for us to stay. It was good to know her true feelings. But whatever love I had left for Steven wasn't strong enough to make us stay. I was determined to book up before China went back to school. Steven desperately tried to convince me otherwise.

"Baby, don't go, we can make this work. Let's give it another go. I love you. It'll be different, I promise," he would say.

With that plea, he even pretended to cry. But it was his reaction afterward that proved me right. Steven hadn't felt too bad about the split, it turned out—he bounced right back. All the griping he'd done, it wasn't long before he was back on the dating scene. Rumor had it that Steven tried to hit on one of my cousins.

For the next person in his life, I would say, "Hip-hop hooray, better you than me!"

In my mission to find a place, it felt like I was banging my head against a brick wall. Luckily, Cousin Lolita, who was separated from her husband, Luke, suggested we stay with her. She lived in a five-and-a-half room apartment with her seven-year-old daughter, Shannon, an only child. As part of our agreement, I'd pay four hundred dollars monthly, and we'd share the room with her daughter. My cousin and I had grown up together—as kids, we spent time together during school breaks and holidays, and we got along well.

As adults, the roommate relationship was a bad move. I was thrilled at first about being roommates, even though I was unsure of how things would pan out. We had different lifestyles and ways of raising our kids. In a very short period, I became frustrated by our different habits. I'd grown to become more of a neat freak when it came to cleaning. My motto was, "A place for everything and everything in its place." Lolita had been more of the opposite: if company was arriving, only then was it time to clean. It was nothing for her to use a dish, leave it in sink, and go to bed. And it wasn't time to clean the fridge until little critters had grown inside the bends.

It was rough and downright scary raising a sick child in such an environment, and Lolita's insensitive attitude toward my daughter drove a wedge into our relationship. On top of that, Lolita thought her daughter, Shannon, was one of Charlie's Angels. But Shannon had become a spoiled, devious little kid. That child had performed every mischievous act under the sun. While China and I had shared the lower bunk bed, Shannon slept in the upper deck, and she had a horrible habit of jumping up and down. After all her treatments, China felt nauseated as she slept on the bottom deck, and the jumping made it worse. In addition, Shannon had a ton of toys scattered about the room, making it hard for us to maneuver. She made our stay even worse by ranting and raving throughout the house. When we watched television, Shannon stood directly in front of the screen and stretched her arms out.

"Would you move from in front of the TV?" China would ask in a low voice.

"No, Mommy's house, and I can do what I want!" Shannon would respond.

With China back at college, I spent time with Peaches as a way to escape the next crisis. Peaches' home had laughter and smiling faces, familiar and unfamiliar. Part of this social circle one night was a memorable face—Greg's. His presence brought back joyous thoughts of the past, and I remembered how we'd parted on a sweet note. It was a great feeling to be among people filled with laughter and joy. We sat on the beige love seat, and Greg talked about the things he'd done. He was still a gentleman, even in his conversation. At the end of the night, we exchanged phone numbers.

The drive home sparked memories of the past. I called and tried to refresh China's memory of Greg.

It didn't work. "Mommy, there's been a few. And it's not clicking. I have to see him to remember," she said.

When China came home, she did little talking and lots of sleeping—it wasn't a good sign at all. Whenever we spoke, she responded angrily, striking back at me in a raspy voice. I'd taken her actions to be a part of mood swings, a sign of her illness. But after three months had passed, the reality of the new situation struck hard.

It was difficult for Dr. Jose to tell us, but he'd always been straight up.

"The cancer cells are back," he told us. "All it took was one little cell to hide while the treatments were at work. This cell could have found any weak spot to attack and reproduce. It's pretty clear this is the case. Now we need to tackle it from a broader approach."

Hearing this, there wasn't a tearless face in the room.

"We must keep trying and hoping," Dr. Jose said.

But only China could make that choice, not either of us.

In her soft, tearful voice, she said, "What's next? Well, will I need radiation or chemo?"

This time it was a whole new ball game. We needed more than chemotherapy or radiation. It was devastating. My thoughts drifted. I thought of God. In no way was I condemning His work nor accusing Him of being unjust, but I needed to speak with Him. In silence, I asked, *Oh, my God, is it ever going to end? Is this the journey we've been chosen to travel?*

I remembered the words "The Lord doesn't give more than you can handle!"

It was there our destiny became clear. Cancer would be a permanent relationship in our lives. Once again, we were patiently listening to our next measures. This time, the treatment was a bone marrow transplant. This method is used when the disease appears to have left after chemotherapy or radiation, but returns shortly afterward.

"South Suburban isn't equipped to deal in bone marrow transplants. You'll need to go where they're medically advanced to treat patients. You'll need to take your medical records with you. I don't work out of that hospital, so I'll see you after the procedure," Dr. Jose told us in a saddened voice.

We had to take on a whole new staff of experts. Our farewell to Dr. Jose left us teary-eyed. As he handed us the medical records, we went onward. The journey here had ended—we had to walk new ground.

The Insight

- Telling a child they have cancer is an emotional challenge for any parent.
- It's best to talk about it from the onset. But as a parent, you must decide the appropriate time.
- Usually, a child knows there's a serious illness, even though discussion is avoided.
- Eliminate the guilt factor—it's not their fault. Let them know they are loved and that there's hope.
- Allow them to express their feelings and emotions. Cue in on their reactions—and embrace.

CHAPTER FIFTEEN

The Marrow Transplant

Our new treatment center at the University of Chicago Hospital was a scary place. The corridors were the longest I've ever seen, with a seemingly endless number of doors going all the way from one end to the next. Even the posted signs were intimidating.

We spent half the morning talking with the doctor assigned to us, Dr. Willis, and her staff. Afterward, there were X-rays and tests to be taken. The consultation with Dr. Willis broadened our perspectives about the bone marrow transplant procedure and its elevated phases, recovery, and discharge stages—a lot to know. Dr. Willis made sure to mention the side effects that could occur: extreme weakness, nausea, vomiting, and diarrhea.

A common approach in the treatment of lymphoma, this procedure restores stem cells destroyed by high doses of chemotherapy or radiation. Without healthy marrow, a patient is unable to produce the blood cells used to carry oxygen, fight infection, and prevent bleeding. A stem cell transplant restores the bone marrow's ability to make the blood cells. We learned about the treatment processes as well: the autologous treatment, in which the patient is her own donor, and the allogeneic transplant, when stem cells are received from somebody else, usually a sibling. Even a person unrelated to the patient may be used. Then there is the syngeneic transplant, in which stem cells are received from an identical twin. In any case, the short-term risks are all similar: nausea, vomiting, fatigue, fevers, feeling depressed, decreased blood counts, loss of appetite, mouth sores, hair loss, and skin reactions. And its long-term effects included infertility, cataracts, and other organ damage.

To minimize the possible side effects, China needed stem cells that closely matched her own, referred to as "human leukocyte antigen typing." The one person we believed could help was her half-sister, Little Barbie, Craig's daughter from Renna. From what we knew, Little Barbie had gotten married and had her own family. So we went on a massive hunt, looking high and low.

Since we knew where Little Barbie once lived, I went over there, knocked on the door, and said, "It's a matter of life and death. We're looking for Little Barbie."

The person at the door replied, "Shucks, she moved away, her been gone. Can't tell ya'll where that was she went, don't know. Sorry, can't help."

Leaving no stone unturned, we tried desperately to locate Little Barbie, but to no avail. Frantic and at my wit's end, I even reached out to her father. Yes, I'd gone to Craig, but it was a wasted effort. He claimed he didn't know her whereabouts either, appearing totally disconnected and uncaring. Not only was that a hard pill to swallow, but I found his news most unbelievable. Inhaling long and deep, I had to take a step back, close my eyes, and slowly count to ten just to refocus my energy elsewhere. Despite how I felt, everything we'd gone through made us stronger. Undoubtedly, China would now be her own donor.

Leading up to the procedure, we were expected to return to the hospital daily. Each visit was necessary to prepare for the conditioning process, since her hospital stay could end up being extensive—thirty to sixty days. This regimen would rid the body of toxic cells and make room for the marrow transplant.

China decided to undertake her journey without delay. The timing was right, with Christmas break less than two weeks away. She was eager and determined to return to school, and she vowed to make a speedy recovery.

For the next three weeks, we were faced with a battery of tests. But no test could compete with the hours China spent on a hospital cot, watching the machine spinning its wheels, draining marrow from her frail body. The harvesting process involved her being hooked up to a machine through a vein port: blood was slowly drawn into the machine, which then syphoned her marrow.

She required some form of anesthesia for the procedure. Since her cells had to be cancer-free, the cells were frozen until ready to be transfused into her body after receiving high doses of chemo. While being treated with doses of anticancer drugs, she received the stem cells through an intravenous line.

This process took several hours. For most patients, this ordeal was unbearably painful. The thought of it all made me woozy and had my stomach tied in knots. But the real suffering would only be known to China.

At the beginning of 1991, China was prepped for the transplant. All those hours of waiting were coming to an end. As she drifted in and out of consciousness, she didn't utter a word. She was drained from all the doses of medicine.

China fought hard to beat the odds. She'd successfully completed phase two of the process and was struggling to enter phase three. China had two days to recuperate. On the third day, she would undergo the final stage. After being treated with anticancer drugs, her harvested stem cells were reinserted to produce new blood cells.

One worry was taken off our shoulders, however. A bone marrow transplant is an incredibly expensive procedure, and most insurance carriers will not cover the cost. We had been blessed—our Blue Cross Blue Shield plan paid for the procedure.

For me, it wasn't easy going to work knowing China was lying in a hospital bed. The sickness flowed from her eyes, and I watched her hair fall out strand by strand, day by day—there was nothing I could do. I fought the tears as I looked at her thin face—she was vain when it came to her hair.

"A woman's glory shines through her hair," China said.

"Your hair falling out is coming from the side effects," I told her.

Surely, she didn't want to hear that reason. The only comfort was for me to be there with open arms. It would take two to four weeks to determine whether the transplant was successful. After the cell infusion, there were precautionary measures that were necessary because of her weakened immune system. China liked the fact that she had a room all to herself. "Now, there they go treating us like VIPs. Boy, look at the size of this room, it's got to cost big bucks," she'd say.

But she didn't have her own room as a luxury. Being susceptible to germs, China had been kept in isolation to minimize potential infections. Anyone who entered the room had to wear a mask. She wasn't even allowed to have live plants. The antibiotic and antifungal medications and blood and platelet transfusions warded off any infections and prevented excessive bleeding. With her system in the danger zone, it could take a year or more to return to normal function.

China made a phenomenal recovery, though. Day by challenging day, China regained her strength. Soon she no longer needed blood or transfusions, and her blood counts returned to normal. The side effects were few to none. A month passed and already China was on her way to being discharged—not many recovered as quickly. Each morning, a glowing sparkle beamed through her eyes.

While in the hospital, China had met another teen girl dealing with this cancerous relationship. The two of them formed a friendship. They'd done a lot of chatting back and forth. China, in her comforting way, rubbed lotion in her palms and gently massaged the other girl's body. Also, she helped her get up to walk around the corridor. Often I found China in the teen's room, giving comfort and support, waiting on her hand and foot—China was a great caregiver. I saw her trying to comb the girl's hair or put a bandana around her head. This was a great thing to observe—to know she wasn't making the journey alone.

Before her discharge, the social services department arranged for nurse visits at home. The nurses provided for China's needs and monitored her progress. It was a delicate process: they maintained the cleanliness of her catheter, took regular blood draws, and checked her vital signs. China remained optimistic: even though it normally took six to eight months to return to a normal level of physical activity, she was already preparing for school.

But the one thing we feared happened.

A few days after China had come home, her new friend's mom called to tell us that the girl had died. "She never got a chance to come home. I just wanted you both to know," her mom said.

What a blow for China! She took the news hard. She became depressed, refusing to talk about it, moping and sleeping for the next few days.

I had other problems to deal with. The nursing care was just the beginning of the road, so I was determined that China would be the responsibility of two of us: me and Craig. So whatever freedom Craig sought would be on hold, I decided. I searched long and hard to find the right lawyer to stand against Craig. Of course, he wouldn't take the intrusion lying down. The courts were the last place he wanted to be.

With the wheels in motion, I moved on to my next project. Since China was now out of the hospital, we needed our own domain. She was edgier with each passing day. Shannon, meanwhile, was constantly in the way and in our faces. It was one of her last capers that put the icing on the cake. When the toilet got clogged up one day, Shannon quickly told everyone: "I didn't do it."

Lolita immediately turned to China and asked, "Why would you stop the toilet up?"

I'd interjected at that point, "My daughter didn't do that. Time we start looking for another place."

I don't recall Lolita's response, but it was agreed that was best for everyone.

China finished her follow-up visits with a series of X-rays. We took the results and went back to Dr. Jose. Another part of the journey had been completed. China had recuperated from her ordeal. No doubt educational goals played a role in that accomplishment. The times I thought she was ready to give up, she came back fighting. China had an abundance of inner strength. She had four months remaining before she'd go back to college.

But she couldn't go down that path until Dr. Jose gave the green light. Once again, we were in his office hoping for a lucky twist of fate—nope, a miracle—for a fulfilled life.

The results revealed it all.

My goodness—oh no, not again! I wanted to scream at the top of my lungs, but I dared not say it out loud. We'd been on one hell of a roller coaster ride that wouldn't stop.

I'd come to the realization that our lives were scripted long before our birth. And so it was our planned destiny to walk alongside this toxic relationship. The only power one truly has is the free will to make decisions after reaching that core path. Those déjà vu moments are life's experiences that have been prewritten.

The look on Dr. Jose's face showed little hope.

"We need to undergo another round of radiation, since some cancer cells remained," he said.

I turned to see anger and disgust on China's face as the tears poured and poured down her cheeks. And crying was something she'd rarely done. Looking at her expressions, I could easily imagine what was going through her mind. It was as though she thought, *All I have gone through, and for what? Was it really worth it? Will I ever beat this disease? I will take control and fight back. I won't let it beat me.*

Was she going to put herself through the process—twelve weeks of rays passing through her frail body? She was determined not to be defeated. It was her way of identifying who had the *control*. No matter what, she would be the one to make another crucial choice. The only stand I took was to be there with love and support. A decision to accept treatment for cancer is a personal choice, and a choice that's neither right nor wrong. At first, her choice was difficult to accept, but I realized it had to be China's pick. And it would be her shoe prints that would lead us on our next journey, not mine.

The Insight

Keeping an open mind: something that's hard to do, but it must be done. Try to understand:

- As adults, we need to see that it's the cancer victim who must take control over his or her treatments measures.
- As caregivers, we need to understand there is no right or wrong.
- When it comes to our loved ones, we must be accepting of their choices.

The implacable judge spoke
harshly, baring no empathy . . .

CHAPTER SIXTEEN

Closing the Gap

Realizing it was time to move on, and with no shelter at hand, I sought to find a place through my sister Dana. She and her husband, Larry, had always been property owners. So if they had a vacant house, it wasn't a problem to rent from them. Dana and Larry were in the business of buying HUD homes and remodeling them. Some they'd keep, and others they'd flip. That was the beauty of it! Larry would do all the repairs himself. It amazed me how lovely the homes looked, especially where he did some major fixing up, like installing siding, gutters, windows, and even some interior finishes.

Frankly, I don't know why I hadn't called Dana sooner. What was I thinking? When we finally spoke, they had recently bought some property, and Larry was working on the repairs. Dana thought it would be a nice house for us. This was a tri-level home with cathedral ceilings, three bedrooms, one bathroom, and a full basement, located in the far suburbs of Markham. After everything China had gone through, this time she'd live in peace and quiet.

Eventually Dana called to tell me, "Larry finally finished the work on the house. We've passed the city's inspection. You'll need to get the water, lights, and gas in your name. That's all it'll take for you to move in."

And after getting settled into the new place, I was determined to continue the court proceedings with Craig.

Meanwhile, as Greg reappeared in our lives, much of the time we spent together revolved around China. I connected emotionally with Greg, inspired by the way he adored China. Perhaps he'd known how draining and stressful things had gotten. Being a caring, dedicated, and responsible person, Greg and China became closely attached. Greg accepted China as a major part of my life. And that itself demonstrated his love for us both. He had been a natural in caring for her, treating her like a princess. When he dropped by, he'd greet her with a smile and make her feel loved. He'd pull the leopard chair to her bedside and read to her—China had been an avid reader. He had a habit of bringing her food, whatever his meal had been. And it seemed he kept a joke or two in his side pocket just to make her laugh. He spent hours sitting and chatting with her. He loved to rent movies and bring them over to watch. Whenever he'd leave, he'd give her a big hug. Stepping up as he had done proved his love for us. China had grown to enjoy his company immensely.

"Mom, he's really a nice guy," she said.

"Well, baby, he sure is," I replied as my eyes watered.

I wanted to turn back the hands of time and wash away that ungodly relationship clinging to her. *I should've been the one chosen. I have lived my life, and I want to possess every toxic cell in her body. She has only begun to live. Her purpose on earth is more meaningful. We all have a purpose in life—so is her mission to bear a disease? And is it mine to walk her through the relationship? Only You know—our God, our Maker, and our Father of the universe.* I don't know why I questioned the situation, because truly, the answer was there.

I didn't have many people to share my crisis with. But this time it would be different—in addition to Greg coming back into our lives, I met a terrific person. She had come from Cincinnati, Ohio, and she was a stranger in a big city where people were cold as breezy winds and snowflakes. I could hardly wait for her to meet China, who would then feel more secure about leaving me behind.

Vernita and I became friends from the start. We initially met on the job. When she walked past in her tailored navy blue suit, she stepped tall and with confidence. Once our eyes connected, she gave a huge smile, and I smiled back.

She must be new. Why is she smiling so? It's a cold city with cold people, I thought to myself.

Before long, we'd struck up a friendly conversation. We decided to have lunch, during which we exchanged our stories. By the end of it, we had become buddies.

No wonder she walked so confidently: she was a war vet. Huh—a manager with no kids, while I had my sick daughter and baby-daddy drama. But we both lived in the suburbs. With the long drive to and from the city, I was so happy to have found a colleague to carpool with. My new friend and I took turns, and I discovered one great trait in her: she was a stickler for time. Being conscientious about things like that myself, I think that was what clinched our relationship. For sure, we were never late for work. And that forty-minute drive gave us plenty of time to get engrossed in chit-chat and really lowered my stress level. Afterward, we'd never let a day pass where we didn't talk.

But as we both had busy lives, we rarely hung out socially. Although, the times Vernita's mom came up from Ohio, they made sure to invite us for some delicious home cooking. As we'd chow down, it gave China and me an opportunity to escape our toxic world. It also gave China a chance to spend some enjoyable moments with another family. And without fail, whenever Vernita's mom baked her old-fashioned sweet potato pies, there was always a pie to take home. We'd hang out until China couldn't hold up any longer. China would say, "Mum, that's good eatin'!" We'd chuckle on the road home.

Not only did this bring back memories of my relationship with Mandy, it gave my heart joy to see China and Vernita bond. Vernita may not have shared every single detail about herself, and neither had I. But as my carpool buddy and friend, who she was had been clearly represented, and I returned the gesture.

This pleasant existence was not to last long, however. It had been two months with China back at school studying freshman pre-law when I received a frantic call. I barely understood her as she cried out, "Mommy! Can I please come home? I can barely walk, it hurts so badly. I promise I won't ask to come back until I'm better."

Right away, I bought her a ticket for the next train. It would be the fastest and quickest way home. I had few words as she stumbled off the train. It had taken lots of energy to hold back tears, watching her go from walking, to stumbling, and then to crawling at the Homewood Station. Truly, the disease had brought her to her knees. And all I wanted to do was fall to mine and plead to God that He'd give me this disease and not her. 'Cause it broke me down seeing how it destroyed my baby. But the only resort was to call Dr. Jose.

I'd hardly spoken a word when he said, "The side effects have taken over. We need to admit her to the hospital. And I'll meet you there."

This time I couldn't hold back the tears. While I let them flow, my thoughts screamed, *Oh my baby, my poor child, your disease is full-blown.* Just to see it full-force would have broken down any parent.

China spent the next two weeks at South Suburban Hospital, fighting back. There was no way of knowing how long she'd be hospitalized, but everything she owned was at school. We needed to move hard and fast. Vernita and I drove the long haul to bring home her belongings, closing the gap. For now, her school dreams would become a closed chapter. To sanction that closing, Dr. Jose even sent a letter to the school, dated May 1, 1992.

It was his last paragraph that let us all know the ending had neared: *". . . is suffering the effects of the chemotherapy, besides having to deal with the effects of her cancer. She is, by any standards, in a desperate situation, fighting for her life . . ."*

The doors opened wide as Craig and I stood in the courtroom. There seemed to be no mercy to relinquish his degree of support. The implacable judge spoke harshly, baring no empathy as she increased his payments—and made him liable for past medical bills. Even though I'd kept health coverage, the out-of-pocket expenses had mounted.

No one should go without insurance in a crisis like this if at all possible. All the different barriers created a mound of medical expenses. The transplant had exceeded $120,000 just for the hospital stay. This didn't cover treatment expenses, meds, or any basic procedures, not to mention the other cancer treatments. I was under a huge financial strain because at eighteen, China required a special dispensation from the insurance carrier. This is the course parents must typically take when their child reaches eighteen. Still, I had my out-of-pocket expenses to fulfill.

Well, I didn't escape from my own share of court demands. Since Craig had HMO carriers, the judge requested that I switch providers. If I did not change, I would have to absorb all future expenses. And before we left, I was court-ordered to provide Craig with our new address. Still, it was decided that we would come back in November, giving Craig time to add her to his insurance. I was determined not to put China through a massive examination or the probing hands of an unfamiliar doctor. Dr. Jose was all we knew and trusted.

"Baby, the judge told me you'd have to change doctors. But don't worry; I'm not going to put you through that. Whatever price Dr. Jose charges, he'll stay as your doctor," I told China.

"Okay, do you think so?" she said, sighing in agreement.

Over the years, China had longed for her father's love and presence as though she worshipped the ground he walked on. As a matter of principle, I had vowed not to speak against him—something parents should never do. Beware: no matter how rotten they've been, their true being comes to light. And that's a fact! China kept an open heart and would accept Craig whenever he would return—she thought the world of him.

We had an incredibly strong bond, too. As we embraced each other one day, she murmured, "Mommy, I won't leave you because there won't be anyone to watch over you. It's you and I against the world." Her promising words comforted my ears.

Those words shall long be remembered. It was a powerful, strong message to hear, and I'll always cherish it.

By the weekend, China received a long-overdue call. As she sat with a wide grin, I knew it was the love of her life—the baby's daddy, Craig. But China didn't feel comfortable seeing her father. She feared her love wouldn't be reciprocated—her physical appearance had drastically changed.

"Mommy, I know—I'll wear my bandana, perk myself up, and smile just for him," she said. Wow, as she spoke those words, it brought tears to my eyes!

Over the next week, China was distant as she waited, barely speaking a word. Once Craig came, life began to emerge from China. When he slowly entered the room, she got a gleam in her eyes and a smile on her face. His visit remained between the two of them. I didn't want to hear what was spoken behind those doors. Finally, Craig reappeared at the staircase and stood there teary eyed, with sadness buried in his heart—or was that guilt? Regardless, I saw tears flow down his cheeks.

When he reached me at the last step, he said, "I can't stand to see her suffering like that. You've done a great job raising our daughter. She makes you proud, huh? You've acquired great strength in coping with it all. She's really tough in dealing with this."

None of those words were what I needed to hear. Perhaps it had been guilt he possessed. But I wouldn't deprive China of his presence.

Each visit brought them closer. China became more vibrant, longing for his acceptance. Craig was finally prepared to take a role in her life. He wanted to be with her as she attended monthly office visits. That was good news! Of course, I was not about to turn down his proposal. For years, I'd struggled alone. Suddenly, I wasn't alone to cope with a ruthless diseased relationship.

China's night sweats were becoming more frequent. Her temperature went to 103 degrees, and we were in and out of the hospital. She had us both guarding her bedside—Craig on one end and me on the other. The hospital became a home away from home for us after work. Many times, we'd sit silently, pretending to watch television, drowning in our own thoughts. There was one common denominator among us—the air China inhaled as it lessened with each breath. Of course, Craig only endured so much. My nights and weekends were spent alone at the hospital, by her side. I lay on the cot with my eyes open, just staring at China.

She tossed and turned for sleep. She moaned and groaned.

She needed sleep so the pains would pass away. We looked forward to spending time together, but she wasn't thrilled about getting visitors. The time we shared was truly precious.

It hasn't been easy to forget one particular Saturday when an unwanted, uninvited coworker crept into China's room like the slimy snake she was. Out of the blue, Emily, a manager from my work, popped her nosey, busybody self in. Her reputation had always preceded her. She was a complete gossiper and nuisance—always in everybody's business. Heck, we weren't close or anything, so why did she stick her nose in our circle? She was an outsider in our life. I hadn't included my own mother in the fight with this diseased relationship.

So it was simple as that—we didn't need Emily dipping and creeping in our affairs. China and I had lived our lives privately. If we'd wanted visitors, I would have sent a call out or posted a bulletin. Of all people, Emily was the last thang we needed snooping about. This was our private circle, ours alone. But the nerve, the audacity—she'd even invited others to come with her. I could see it in China's eyes—she wanted them to vanish like lightning. We'd always been able to key in on each other's body language. I could read China's thoughts: *Why are you all here? I don't want to see you, nor want you to see me. Why won't you leave? Leave! Leave now!*

I didn't say anything at first, but I was fuming, fuming, fuming! We all sat around the room. China felt uneasy and uncomfortable, so all the other visitors who had compassion got up and left. You'd think Emily would feel the same emotion, but she didn't budge. She wasn't going to, either. I couldn't stomach to look at her any longer. She hung around, sucking up our quality time and gossiping about everything that went on around the job.

So eventually, I told her, "We need to leave the room. Let her rest. Let's walk."

I'd paid no attention to all her gossip, but the last thing she said hit a nerve and lit a flame: "Did the doctors tell you how much longer she has? I want you to know I'll be there to help with the funeral arrangements, when it's time."

How dare she talk to me about that! Straight out, I nipped it in the bud and said, "You need to leave. I'm serious, leave right now. And don't bother to come back!"

It was as though I had to force her out of our lives. It took long enough, but that mouse crawled into her hole. She left. The shoe prints we'd made were for our journey alone. (*Remember: it's not a good feeling to be in the presence of someone who makes you uneasy in your own space, castle, domain, or however you'd classify it.*)

The Insight

Unwanted visitor(s) can certainly make your experience worse:

- The unwanted visitor brings negative forces. And that's something a person doesn't need while coping with an illness.
- The unwanted visitor doesn't appear only when a disease returns. The unwanted visitor can also be the person(s) who invades your circle.
- The unwanted visitor is a person who has the power to ruin your mood—if you allow them. And they'd be your worst enemy.

CHAPTER SEVENTEEN

Final Dazes—The Homecoming

As I wrote about this portion of our journey, I found myself pushing through a painful moment in time. But I knew this too would pass as our shoe prints traveled to the homecoming. It's an important piece to share.

China was readmitted to South Suburban Hospital after having been released. The fear of losing her bonded our family. Many a night, the nurses came in the room to probe their needles deep into her flesh. No matter how hard they tried, the blood that flowed through her tiny veins no longer surfaced. There she lay in a hopeless, lifeless state. The blood that dried up in her veins now filtered through her urine. The catheter bag hanging from the tubes bore a deep flush of redness. Her struggle to end it all weighed heavy on her mind. As her temperature rose to 108 degrees, she cried out: "Mommy, I don't care anymore. So many things wrong with me—bumps under my neck and arms, sores on my back, I'm falling apart. I don't care if I never get out. Just let me die here. Mommy, I'm serious."

I wanted no part of this defeat—I felt she had to go on fighting. We'd come too far to throw away the years. My thoughts questioned, *Has she finally had enough of the suffering and struggle? Is she ready to give up?*

The next week was breathtaking. One day, at about 1:15 p.m., I got the call to come to the hospital. Seeing no light, I hit the panic button and called Craig, who worked only a few blocks away. When I finally arrived, my heart skipped a beat. Motionless, I stood glancing at the sign that read Intensive

Care Unit. As his eyebrows raised and lips sagged down, I realized the sadness Craig felt. He was huddled over her, his head hung low, peering down upon her fragile body. The whole room was filled with a scent of sickness. While I held back the tears, I watched the machines pump life into her tiny body. As each doctor conjured up his own prognosis, survival turned into a relationship with death.

Death felt so pervasive that the priest came and gave the last rites. As he leaned over the bed and lowered his head, he prayed, ". . . His holy oil and great goodness of mercy, may God . . ."

By the time the priest had left, my heart was torn into a million pieces. My world crushed before my eyes. I became terrified and saddened. I shook my head and rubbed my tongue against the roof of my mouth.

As I continued to grasp the soggy, crumpled-up tissue in my hand, I thought, *That's a lie. My baby angel has not left.*

With my head spinning, I gaped down at her lifeless body. There would be no goodbyes, only hellos. While I looked helplessly at my little angel, I geared my mind and heart into a mode of motherly love.

I reached over and took the covers to pull back, cuddled her in my arms, and rested her against my bosom.

"My little angel, you're sleeping so heavily. Time to wake! Wake up now. I carried you those nine months while you kicked inside," I whispered in her precious ear.

I tickled her tiny chin, stroked her soft, baby-fine hair that had grown back after chemo, and pressed her cheek to mine. "Don't you feel my heart pounding? I'm giving you life. I love you, and I want you to come home," I said, sobbing.

As I continued to quietly weep, my voice got shaky. "Remember, you promised you wouldn't leave me," I whispered. "I know Mommy hasn't done everything right in life. I wanted so badly to safeguard you from this disease. I'm so sorry. Forgive me, my angel." I apologized over and over while I cried, holding her hands in mine.

I'd become a total wreck seeing my baby lying lifelessly. I wrapped my arms around that frail body and pulled her into a hug. She felt like nothing but skin and bone. But she was my skin-and-bone baby child, and I caressed her with my body.

What happened next was shockingly and gratifyingly amazing!

Her voice sounded like a cry of the dead. She inhaled a deep breath and proclaimed the words, "Oh, no, not the water! The water is too cold—take me back, take me back! Mommy said it's not time to come home!"

She then shook her head as though her body became afloat. Slowly her eyes opened and she murmured, "Whoa, whoa, what happened? Where was I? Mommy, why are those people up there laughing at me?"

I darn near froze right then and there. The reality set in, and it was all I could do to curl up and sob.

My Lord and Savior brought her back to me, I thought.

There was a great deal of comfort and lots of sadness. I was sad and happy at the same time. Saddened that I'd actually lost her, but happy God had given her a second breath of life. I found joy in my life to have gotten her back.

I completely melted after hearing her words. It was an added joy as I smiled through the tears. The people she'd asked about were angels—the ones laughing. They along with my Savior sent her back. It had been the amazing power of prayer. China said she wasn't ready, they listened, and He allowed her to return.

I realized the return was to prepare me for her transition. That was a preparation no parent may ever accept, but must learn to cope with.

On the third day, China made an amazing 180-degree turn. All the symptoms that had placed her in intensive care lessened, and she was moved to a regular room. It was very puzzling—none of the doctors had an answer.

"How is it that her condition changed so rapidly?" I asked.

"I can only say it's a miracle! The odds are astronomical. Her condition reaches beyond any medical science," one doctor responded.

Once she became stable, China was moved to a regular floor. She spent a week there. But Monday, November 2, 1992, wasn't only a time for gearing up for the election of our forty-second president, with Bill Clinton running for office. It was also the day we found out China's body was shutting down.

She would spend the rest of her time at home. With social services working to set up hospice care, she would be discharged that Thursday. Since she was at a most critical stage, the care providers would focus on her comfort while helping her fully enjoy life. I couldn't wait to tell China that Thursday she would be coming home. As I dashed into the room to tell her about the release date, she challenged the truth.

She cried out, "No, Mommy, Tuesday. Thursday is too long!"

Thinking she misunderstood, I repeated, "No—not Tuesday, but Thursday."

Again she cried out, "No, Tuesday, not Thursday, Mommy!"

I couldn't understand why she was agitated, but I agreed just to please her. There was sadness in my heart as I bent over to kiss her forehead. With this news weighing on my shoulders, I knew the time had come to use some family leave. The Family Medical Leave Act allows an employee to take leave for a personal medical condition or to take care of a new baby or sick family member. Although there is no pay for the time off, it would be leave I was entitled to. So the next day, I'd start the process for this leave.

That night, I drove the long way home. I was consumed by an empty feeling. I didn't care if it was the wee hours; I needed to talk to someone, to anyone. It was deeper than my heart could bear. But I didn't call anyone. I decided to drown my sorrows.

When I got home, I had a strong urge to listen to my favorite song by Mariah Carey, "I Don't Wanna Cry." The melody of Mariah's high-octave vocals embraced my pain and sorrow perfectly, somehow.

I drowned my emotions in a bottle of booze—E & J Cognac, straight. I got lost in the emptiness inside myself. I'd almost lost her. I kept drinking anyway. Could I have sunk any lower?

But the booze didn't lessen the pain. It had truly been one of the worst moments in my life. I'd loved her so, but felt her drifting away. There was this huge void. It felt as though I wanted to give up, just keel over and die before she was gone. It had become so darn hard to live my life. We parents are supposed to go before our children! The sadness and loneliness felt unbeatable.

"Why won't you take away my pain? Take away this pain! Would you?!" I screamed to my God.

Emotionally drained and taxed, I became completely burned out. The booze didn't help it any. On top of those emotions, there was a burning pain in my chest that refused to leave. As I sipped the last of the liquid from my glass, I threw my head back, forced open my eyes, and, looking up at the ceiling, I asked my God, "Shall I ever find contentment and peace inside?" But I felt no escape. This diseased relationship had finally swallowed us up.

I felt the thing to do was to call Dawn. We worked at the same job, and my sister Dana had orchestrated Dawn and me being close friends. Dana's persistency cemented our bond.

With our busy and hectic lifestyles, I had no intention of drawing Dawn into our toxic world. For one, she had her social circle and I had mine. While my world had been full of toxicity, she was focusing on nurturing her wholesome family. The bit I knew about Dawn was that she'd met her Prince Charming on the job. He had been wooing her so, and she'd given in and gotten hitched.

Even though he was her second husband, he had been with Dawn since her four children were very young. Through the years, they had grown to love and admire him as a dad—not just as a stepfather. For her second time around, she married a man with loving, caring, and nurturing qualities. He was a real homebody kinda guy. You know the kind, who loves taking family trips, eating together, and gathering for TV time. His ole Southern gentleman traits made him more special. And when it came to Dawn, he nurtured her every whim, whatever that may have been. To say the least, he had treated her like a Caribbean Queen. She married the type of husband many of us single women looked to snatch up.

To those who knew her, Dawn was a praying woman, full of wisdom and knowledge.

And that night I needed a prayer partner. When I called, she was asleep. Even in her sleepy mode, she wanted to hear the latest news about China. Breaking through the sniffles and tears, I poured my heart out. Once I told her about the hospice and about China's responses, she listened and then responded with words of wisdom.

"We just need to hold onto our faith and belief."

Before we hung up, she recited the Lord's Prayer.

In that moment, it was her words that provided me with comfort and ease.

The next morning, I could hardly keep my eyes open. With all that had happened, it was time to face society.

Truly, I didn't know why I bothered to go to work that day. Wearing a plastic smile only camouflaged the real world I was living in. Once I got to work, I contacted the hospital. "She had a rough night, but is resting peacefully now," the nurse responded.

The news made me sigh with relief. I was working in management then, and I was scheduled for off-site supervision. When that occurred, I'd have to leave the building to spend an entire day on the streets monitoring an employee's performance, wherever the location might be.

I left my peers holding down the fort, I thought.

But by the end of the day, my thoughts would be far from work. What mouse-faced Emily did on that particular day hasn't been easy to forget.

By early morning, several calls had come in from the hospital. While I was on street duty, Emily had taken those calls. Each had appeared to be more urgent than the last, requesting that I come immediately. Emily never relayed the messages to me.

Job procedures in place at our work clearly dictated that should a person receive an emergency call, all possible attempts were to be made to locate them. Emily robbed me of the protection that rule provided to employees.

Many questions have chipped at my mind ever since. How cruel and heartless could one person be? What possible motive could she have for such an act? Would I ever open my heart to look past her actions? Or was it that only God held the answers?

It was after 2 p.m. when I finally got back in the building. To my surprise, my coworkers began to come up and offer condolences. No one could fathom the state that threw me into. Even more shocking were those messages stacked in the middle of my desk, taken by Emily, all noting that the hospital had called. I feared returning the calls. The notes indicated that they'd started early that morning.

I called the nurse back. She immediately became upset that I hadn't responded earlier.

"Where have you been? Come, come quickly!" she yelled into the phone.

I dropped everything to look for Vernita. I needed her to take me to the hospital. Once I found her, we quickly left the building, when Emily ran out behind us.

"Wait, I'm going with you too!" she yelled out after us.

"You'd better get her back!" I shouted to Vernita, while leaping to grab hold of Emily.

What kind of person was Emily—dipping all in my business? We were dealing with it in a private, personal circle. It had not been work-related. Vernita knew this and held her back.

The extent of Emily's interference was even worse than we had thought.

When Vernita and I arrived at South Suburban Hospital, a nurse greeted us.

"You've come. We've been calling you all day. We'd spoken with your sister," a nurse said.

As she mentioned her name, I angrily replied, "Oh no, what are you talking about? She's not my sister!"

"Well, that's what she said. So, we told her about your daughter and asked her to locate you," the nurse responded.

Emily had actually told the nurse she was my sister so that she could find out more. What an incredible lie! What a boundary she'd crossed! Believing that bald-faced lie, the nurse shared details about my daughter that were reserved for my ears and my ears only. My God, my God, unbelievable Emily had gone that far. It was outrageous enough that Emily would tell such a lie. But not to have notified me drove me into a frenzy.

When we walked toward China's room, a cold wave passed through my body. On approaching the door, I noticed it was shut.

"Why, why is the door closed?" I yelled out.

No one answered. Obviously, they had their reason. I entered the room. China's eyes were closed, and her face possessed a heavenly glow. Although

China had been gone for some time, her body had been untouched. Embracing her, I felt that her body temperature had dropped—the touch of her skin was cold as ice. All of us in the room, including Craig, gathered around her lifeless body.

"My baby, oh, my precious baby!" I screamed as I cuddled her to my bosom.

The nurse came in several times to let us know that they needed to remove China's body. Seeing not a dry eye in the room, she walked out every time, dropping her head. China lay peacefully, with a smile on her face, her complexion clear and blemish-free—fresh and smooth as a baby's flesh. I could not let her go. When the nurse finally came to remove her, it was Craig who pried our bodies apart.

Yes, it was Tuesday, November 3, 1992: the day William Jefferson Clinton won the presidential election, and the Tuesday that China wanted to leave. It was 1:05 p.m. when she returned home.

Amazingly, I realized, she had actually known it would be her time. I clearly remembered her words from the previous day or the day before: "No, Mommy, Tuesday. Thursday is too long!"

I thought she had meant coming back to our home. That had been a mistake. She meant the home from whence she came, our Heavenly Pearly White Gates. She was freed, freed from the diseased relationship, the pain, the struggle, and the evil that had hovered around her in this dark, cruel world. Finally, China was free to live a better life. Throughout her relationship with that disease, she was recognized as having a heart of oak.

As free as China was, my thoughts were not all about relief, far from it. No parent should ever have to bury his or her child. The pain (the ever-intensifying pain!) is unlike anything ever experienced and just breaks your heart. For a parent, the ordeal is totally unbearable. And a parent can literally lose his or her freaking mind. Over the years, the pain never, ever leaves—it only softens.

After China had left, I recalled those words from our Heavenly Father: "Leave, and I'll be with you."

The guardian angels stayed beside us until it was time for God's child to return. Finally, my China got the Father relationship she deserved.

God had given me an opportunity to live a life as a loving and caring parent—for that, I'm truly blessed. Not every person gets the chance to be a parent, and having been one, I'm grateful. I lost her at such an early age. She was just twenty-one years young. When was the last time we (as parents) told our children how much we loved them? That's something to think about, huh? I lost my little angel to another life. She's left me with many precious memories. But I've found everlasting peace and comfort in knowing the toxic relationship was over, and she'd earned her wings. So, through its string of heartfelt words, I gift my poem: *My Little Angel.*

My Little Angel, you're gone now
Gone to a place where other Angels will show you the ropes
Learn all you can from 'em to quickly earn your wings
Sure, this old world was a destructive place to have lived
But you're free, as free as an eagle, the sky, the moon, and
     the sun
No more worries, no more meds, no more fighting the toxic
     diseases
And all those ugly things that living here does to one.

My Little Angel, you're starting life freshly anew
You have an eternal life and such a glorious life
You're back home, from whence He sent you to me
When we were introduced, I was known as a Mommy figure
I named you, raised you, and gave you all my love
Mommies don't really know it all, but I did the best I knew.

My Little Angel, now that you're back home, remember
I'll always embrace your existence on this earth and cherish
     its memories
I couldn't have prayed for a greater child than you
Our paths have parted, but that which we shared lives forever.

My Little Angel, life on earth doesn't remain the same
Your life was short-lived, and that gave us such little time to
     grow
For now, I'll learn to be brave and begin to relive
'Cause I know we'll reunite in the Hereafter
My Little Angel, just know when I get there, our bond shall
     forge again.

—Mommy

My daughter was my soul mate, my best friend, and meant everything to me. My dreams to see her build a foundation have been scattered. And that safe haven I thought I had at the workplace was ripped apart. The day I lost China, my life turned upside down and inside out.

That whole experience had seemingly sent me to hell and back. I became engulfed by rage, and my depression had finally whacked me out. It meant nothing to curl into a fetal position, with my back curved, head bowed, and all limbs bent and drawn in. I could have stayed that way endlessly.

I'll say this again: parents aren't expected to live to bury their children.

And when they do, the impact can be heartbreaking, devastating. Although the wounds mend, they are never fully healed—especially during holidays, birthdays, graduations, wedding ceremonies, and even when embracing someone else's child or grandchild. In the beginning, the tears flowed outwardly, but later they would flow inwardly.

China had made her transition. In this life, I'll never see her married. Nor be able to help raise a child of hers, as a grandparent.

Eventually, I found some comfort. Certain things did help, like the day the nurse came and said, "I wanted you to know we didn't let her die alone. When it was time, I stayed with her and held her in my arms until the end. I told her how much you loved her and that we all will miss her. For you, I hope this gives some comfort, knowing she wasn't alone."

Although I was grateful, I still longed to be there as a parent. Through all this, I knew I could not let go without making one dream come alive. The mortuary that held her remains was Gatling's Chapel on 101st and Halsted. Dana had picked out the most elegant white and gold casket. There China lay, dressed in a long, white lace bridal gown, wearing pearl earrings with her glossy red lipstick, and looking beautiful as an angel bride. Inside that beautifully white, satin-bedded coffin, I placed her little stuffed animals for comfort as she slept. I knew her beauty lived on as she married into another relationship.

At China's homecoming, Vernita was our mistress of ceremony. There we sat listening to Linc as he sang and played his guitar to that well-known funeral melody, "It's So Hard to Say Goodbye to Yesterday." This beautiful piece was originally recorded by G. C. Cameron. Now with Linc singing it, his vocals rocked the church. The lyrics alone are so electrifying and meaningful.

Linc started out the song by guitar-picking for just a bit. His approach at the beginning of the song was very gentle. And he sang in a genuine and contagious manner, being on key with every note. I felt an emotional and powerful connection. I couldn't help but wrap my heart around its lyrics, even when he held onto a note. With my eyes softly closed, tears rolling down my checks, and my body rocking right to left then left to right, the music drew me in. Sitting there listening to every word, every single line, and every vocal note, I was being taken on an emotional high ride. As the melody flowed, I sank deeper into the words of the song. The tone of his vocals was nothing less than breathtaking. I didn't ever want him to stop singing. It was truly an elegant and appropriate song. And I knew I had found solace through its lyrics.

The way Linc swept me into that song, it was hard to let go of the memories and moments China and I shared. But as we move on, something must be left behind. Even though life is a batch of memories, there are no guarantees when it comes to life. It can be ripped out from under us at any point. So we need to live it to the fullest and give back our love to the max. Hearing that song, I thought about what this meant for me. As the seconds, minutes, hours, days, months, and years pass, I've learned to go on with courage, strength, and hope. After finishing many years of continuous therapy, counseling, and support, I regained China's inner strength—because someday our paths shall cross, and we'll reunite in another life.

Since revisiting our journey at the homecoming, I can still embrace those beautiful words by my young cousin, Wendi. She was only sixteen when she stood up and graciously spoke about how precious their love was—the love she had harbored for China. Over and over, I have found myself reaching back to wrap my heart around those words.

Love Is

Love is feelings of happiness, sorrowfulness, sadness, and blueness . . .
And it's all worth living knowing I'll never love another in the way I've
loved you . . .
Love is those feelings no one else can acquire . . .
And as I embrace these emotions they will always and forever be dear . . .
Love is pouring out those teardrops that fall to weep your passing . . .
Cousin, dearest cousin, my love for you
is never ever having to say goodbye . . .

Perhaps those weren't the exact words, but it is how I've chosen to remember them. So to our cousin Wendi, I salute you for embracing me with a chain of memories.

Those that are here will tell us when their time has come, just as China did. And we should take heed when they speak.

Four years later, in December 1996, Dana made her transition. She had known, and I'd listened. We learned that Dana had been diagnosed with breast cancer. It started in the breast and spread, even though she had various treatments. Despite them, her disease had gone full-blown. It had metastasized in her kidney, liver, and brain. When her cancer cells moved to other body parts, it didn't change the type of diseased relationship; Dana's cancer originated in the breast, and any new growth had been recognized as an extension of the initial diagnosis—for her, that was breast cancer.

During Dana's last hospital stay, I watched as she tossed and turned most of the night. After a shot of pain meds, Dana slowly drifted into a deep sleep, uttering words no one understood. The tears continuously poured down my cheeks, and I slept little that night. When Dana awoke early the next morning, it was like she'd known I had been there—she turned to give me a smile. But before she could say anything, she began to vomit up massive amounts of black liquid. As her breath began to gurgle, she gave a roaring death rattle. Still unbeknownst to our family, Dana had taken her last breath.

I panicked, then quickly reached out and pressed the emergency button. I called the nurses' station. "Oh my God, nurse, nurse, something has happened! She needs you!" I yelled.

The nurse arrived right away and immediately told me that I had to step out.

After leaving the room, I called Larry to let him know. It was at South Suburban Hospital that Dana had made her transition, at 8 a.m. on Tuesday, December 10, 1996.

Afterward, there was only one thing to be said, and I said it to myself: "Although it had been painful to relive the relationship with the disease, I'm thankful I was there during my sister's homecoming—'cause she became another angel who'd gone home."

I was in a fragile state after watching her endure it all. Her pain and suffering had gotten so great that she wanted to return from whence she'd come. My sister—oh, my sister!—I was with her through all the triumphs and defeats of the disease. I remembered the time when she'd called me over to her home and we had a long sisterly talk. Before it ended, Dana had asked me to step into her shoes, to continue to watch over the family. And then she begged me to let her go. I remembered how I'd refused to let China go, but I'd had to allow her to leave. Dana, too, was ready to go.

To hear those words again was heartbreaking in itself—it flooded me with memories of China, her suffering, and all that a disease can do. As painful as it was, Dana had asked for acceptance before leaving, and I gave it even though I had not been ready. Really, when is one ever ready to accept a loved one's passing?

Well, the two most adored people of my life, China and Dana, have made their transition after a relationship with the Big C. Yet while with us, they brought their gifts and we embraced them. Dana had been our family's bonding strength. After her passing, the bond broke between us siblings. The one sibling I remain close to is my brother Bobby.

Life had many more obstacles and many twists and turns. In December of 2010, some fourteen years after Dana had passed, Netti too became a victim of this diseased relationship. Her battle for life was short-lived. It was as though the cancer had formed overnight and destroyed her within five months. But through the imprints of her shoe prints, Netti had found her way back—from whence she'd come. Keeping a positive attitude, she never lost faith and accepted her journey. Another balloon was released, and we sent another angel home. Netti, too, shall be remembered as a trooper. As a result, the cycle, the battle, the memories, and the shoe prints—they all resurfaced.

Mom, too, has found peace. It was her time to go. She's in a much better place—a place where she could join her father, mother, sisters, brothers, husband, daughter, granddaughter, grandson, and many other relatives and friends.

(Let me revise that. I'm not sure which home her husband went to. But I can only hope it was Heaven.) Anyway, Mom's homecoming was on Thursday, March 30, 2000, at 7:52 a.m.

Ora Bea, too: the day she met her maker was Friday, May 10, 2013. It's been said that if you can't say something positive, don't say anything at all. And I'll leave it at that.

My dear friend Mandy: this angel was removed senselessly by her estranged husband. Baylee removed this angel. The reason had been a selfish one—he'd gotten fed up with her bringing the kids to his job and asking for child support money. It just goes to show that we'll never know how or when the shoe prints of a journey will end.

But we all bear gifts. And looking at all those angels who were sent to shower us with their gifts, I can only be grateful to have known them all. So, when a person comes into your life, don't question their existence—just embrace their presence. Take it from the Holy Father: they are there for a reason, and we must embrace that moment. It was a lesson learned through the shoe prints of our journey.

My relationship with Greg ended after China's demise. There was no unpleasant or apparent reason for our parting—I just needed to deal with my own inner feelings. At the time, there wasn't room for anyone else in my heart, even though Greg wanted to be at my side. And I know this for a fact, because Dawn told me what he had said to her: "I loved them both so much. But I don't know how to help her now. How can I help her, tell me?" Greg had said this and more as the tears poured down his cheeks, Dawn told me. To know that he'd gone to Dawn and confessed his true love about us is so meaningful. And for that, I'll always be grateful and will hold a place for him in my heart.

And here's a twist for y'all: Renna turned the tables and had a fling during her marriage to Craig, and vowed to make Craig responsible for the child she'd birthed. But Craig wasn't even the child's biological father. That news was a lot to swallow! It's been said that what you put in the wash comes out in the rinse. Or how about this one: what you dish out comes back at ya? Does this hold true in Craig's case? You be the judge.

With China no longer a connecting force between us, Craig had moved on. He divorced and got a new family. After a few years, he retired and began living a comfortable, fruitful, and prosperous lifestyle in a small suburban city where he resided with his new wife and adopted son. Yeah, he'd really done it—went and adopted his new wife's son! Anyhow, the little he'd done for his own daughter wasn't that he didn't know better. He just chose not to do better. That's something Craig must deal with in this life. It doesn't take much to be a seed donor, but it takes a real man to be a dad. Figuratively speaking, he's only the baby daddy, and that label fits him well.

As for Larry, he'd hung in the circle of this disease and stayed until the finish. That says a lot about him as a husband! For the love he showed my sister Dana, he'll always have a place in my heart as Brother-in-law with a capital B. Larry eventually remarried and gained a new family, living in a suburban city. He and his new wife had opened their hearts and decided to raise all their grandchildren, Larry with his own two grandchildren and his wife's three grandkids. They united as one big family. Their children are very loving, and they've recognized each other as sisters and brother. Brother-in-law still works the side-trade rehabbing houses, in addition to his day job.

Of all the friends I thought would remain close to me, Peaches would have been the one. No one could've told me that she wasn't my BFF, but if they did, they would have been right. We've gone our separate ways and are no longer friends.

During my grieving period, Peaches spoke some words that pierced my heart. It had only been about four weeks after China's death, and I was all alone in my home, depressed and overwhelmed with sorrow. The grief had just overflowed within me. I was in such a daze and in a completely zoned-out state. I felt as if my heart had become dislocated from the rest of my body. Having not bathed for weeks, I had a terrible body odor, my hair stood straight up on top of my head, and I'd worn that same funky gown for weeks on end. I walked throughout the house crying out loud and screaming at the top of my lungs as if I was in the midst of a temper tantrum. Even though the phone rang numerous times, I refused to answer. The time I looked at the caller ID and seen it had been Peaches, I didn't bother to stop crying. I picked up the receiver and barely said hello, sobbing into the mouthpiece.

Without hesitation, Peaches yelled, "She's gone now! You just need to get over it and move on with your life!"

My God, she didn't even say hello. Her words immediately jabbed deeply and ripped my heart. Yes, the heart that I'd felt I'd lost.

"Forbid you ever lose a child! You called my house; I didn't call yours. Don't ever call again!" I yelled hysterically and slammed the phone down. We have not spoken since, even after all these years.

But perhaps time shall heal all wounds.

Until a person's shoe prints have marked the entire journey, it's best to avoid such a phrase. Once spoken, it will be remembered for a long time. Of all the people in our circle, I never thought Peaches would have spoken those words.

Vernita and I are still close. After China's homecoming, she returned to her hometown in Ohio. But despite it, we communicate regularly and visit each other. Since her retirement, she enjoys living a comfortable and fruitful life.

As for Dawn, we're close as well. She too had retired and relocated to another state, where she lives a happy and carefree life. After many years,

Dawn divorced her Prince Charming. She chose to live the single lifestyle with her children grown and gone. But to have married him, she was truly blessed. We still see each other regularly.

This time, reflecting back, it's a Minnie Riperton moment: her music video clip "Memory Lane" plunges deep into the soul.

Uh-huh, whenever I hear the words, I get all choked up and teary eyed, 'cause it does move one down their own personal memory lane. Embracing Minnie's lyrics brings me to recapturing my daughter's shoe prints. It was as though she too *"Didn't want to go . . . Wanted to be saved . . . Had it to attack all over again . . . "* and each time we thought it was over, *"It all came back with the quickness of sound . . ."* Surely, patients that relapse into the disease can relate to its original tune. The words, by this perfect angel, and her vocal range will take anyone back down memory lane, on all levels.

Now, when I think of Minnie, she left us when she was only thirty-one years young in 1979, with so much left to offer. Like China, who died at twenty-one, thirteen years later in 1992, they both had lived only through their tender years of life. These two angels were sent from above to touch us with their gifts. It only proves that to have taken our angels, cancer is a killer, a diseased relationship, and it *must* be wiped out.

China was my daughter, my heart, my soul mate. We'd weathered so many storms. Her struggles, hopes, and dreams had ended for us all.

But thinking about China's death also brings back the memory of Emily stepping in to divide us. As a parent, I have said to myself many times, "I should have been there."

When China took her last breath, I never got the chance to be at her side.

Emily had taken away that time and some precious moments. We didn't say our farewells, nor talked about her leaving, the life after, our good times, places we'd been, and everything endured. We had a lot to talk about, and Emily made that impossible. Not only was I profoundly broken by what happened, there had to be some pain for my daughter, being left without her mom. Just how could Emily be so heartless and cruel? A person that cruel and inhumane is truly one morbid individual. Her actions made me feel raped inside and out. No wonder my mind had been damaged.

My mind had been damaged, so I went stark raving mad.

Through the years, others told me, "Girl, I know you wanted to do some real harm to her."

And they were darn tootin'! How's wringing her skimpy neck while ripping the rest of her body apart?

I even imagined burning her at the stake. How about slowly chopping her to shreds while cutting her heart from its socket? When thought out, there were an abundance of ways to return the pain. But no torture could repair what had already been inflicted on me. Through the years, I became one traumatized, sickened, damaged, whacked-out, crazed, screwed-up, and messed-up individual. Those toxic thoughts were never played out and are buried deep in my mind. The toxic world I once lived in was pitch black and so full of darkness. Now all that toxicity has become a thing of the past. Truly, I've experienced what "sufferance" looks and feels like and have come to realize that God takes care of His wounded children. We live protected by His hands.

> A word of caution: When you are at your most vulnerable, never let your guard down. Remain alert to those who squirm their way into your environment. Avoid the creepers who prey. Circle yourself only with those who are protectors of your haven. These things will help you maneuver through the healing relationships.

What pleasure could Emily have found in depriving someone from being with her dying child? Maybe she can peacefully live with herself. I'll never understand her motives or actions for robbing me of the one person who had brought joy to my life and given me a reason for living. Early on, I'd felt confident that Emily's judgment day would come. It's not within my power to punish. But what she deserves comes from the hands of a higher being. It's been said that karma comes back at you two-fold. Guess what—there's some truth to that!

It happened in 2005: Emily got her just desserts after sticking her nose in somebody else's business again. That time she went down fast. Before the job could lower the axe (it's my slang for the office firing her), she ran like the dickens and resigned. Frankly, I don't want to give this too much energy. So moving on, I'll leave the chips where they've fallen. But it does give me some pleasure in exposing that bit of information.

———

And now that you've traveled our journey, can you see how we've climbed so many hills and mountains? Do you want to ask me what part of the cycle was the most difficult?

I'd probably answer three things: 1) holding back the tears—because you must never let them see you cry, 2) letting go of an angel who had a relationship with you, and 3) watching death take its course when ain't a darn thing you can do about it.

There are two gifts that had made life real and precious: unconditional love and support. Without those gifts, her loss would have come sooner. Yet not to have lost her at all, I'd have given my life. Perhaps there are blessings to be cherished from the times we'd shared. But for me, it hadn't been enough— God had lent her only for a while. And I need the lifespan of an eternity to fill that void.

In remembrance of China's suffering, I must move forward, though our love will never be changed. Her relationship with a disease shall not go in vain. Her voice speaks out! There is nothing secret about a diseased relationship. It's a silent scream to many, and its weapon of death must be destroyed. Those imprints, those shoe prints that made the journey—they all ended here.

We have a dream and some hope left. It's our *dream* that we'll band together and strike back, and hope that this disease shall one day be taken out of relationships, and that we'll learn to recognize toxicity early on. Cancer doesn't care about the color of our skin, our educational, economic, or religious background, our age range, or our gender. That relationship was borne to destroy our bodies! While my daughter endured this relationship, the stand I chose to take was a symbolic one. At the time, I cut off all my hair—to the bare scalp.

But now I live to speak about the shoe prints that took us through this relationship and other toxic elements. For me, it's a way to take a stand, speak out, and strike back. And when I think of my daughter, I pay tribute to all of those who are also fighting toxic relationships: Know you are not alone. We stand beside you!

The Insight

Treasure the lost loved one: cherish the memories and embrace his or her presence. These are some coping mechanisms:

- Write or journal about the journey.
- Establish a memorial in honor of your loved one.
- Make a donation in honor of your loved one.
- Volunteer for a cause.
- Create a fundraiser for the cause.
- Donate books to libraries in honor of your loved one.

Remember, our life is designed with no dress
rehearsals. We get . . .

Finding Peace and Comfort

A s our journey ends, there's comfort in writing this poem for my Little
Angel and for all the others who have fought toxicity.

> Dearest child, you didn't deserve
> To endure that battle
> Your life had only just began
> So, don't know why things had gone apart
> Just know: as parents we'll continue far
> As we fight and carry your torch
> 'Cause someday we'll change the course
> Together then we'll rejoice
> And embrace that one day when
> **We can shout for joy over our Victory!**
>
> *—Mom*

Having come this far, you've traveled alongside our shoe prints. Yes, it has
been difficult to cope, but I've finally found peace and comfort through it all.

I had put my job first rather than staying home with my daughter during
her crucial and critical days. Once I realized that, the guilt ripped completely
through me.

Actually, I lost my freakin' mind and found myself stuck in a traumatized state for years. As a dreamer, I wrapped all my thoughts around having a nuclear family and around the battle to overcome a diseased relationship. Pretending it all never existed, I lived a lie and refused to accept the truth. But while I was living in denial, there had been one truth: I had to face reality. It happened, and it was real—she died.

It took years to discover how damaging grief could be. That one word can destroy every living organ in your body. It can gobble you up quickly. The loss of a loved one can be enough to make life a painful endeavor. That's a journey no one should travel alone, nor have it swept under the rug for them. Through continuous therapy, I discovered it had been China's courage that helped me to realize my inner strength.

There's ample support to help us in alleviating the aches and pains. But when we made our shoe prints on the journey, those support systems were not used, because cancer was our family secret and not a topic for discussion. The attack of this toxic relationship can be a heavy cross to bear. Even for those not physically afflicted by the disease, the mental effects are just as damaging. So whether you're the patient, a family member, or a friend, know that the reach is widespread.

When seeking out support groups, transportation services, disease information, grant money for patients, financial assistance programs, nutritional food lists, fundraising information, spiritual support, medical advice, or whatever else you might need or want, know that there are places to meet these needs.

There's so much we experienced as we made the shoe prints. On our journey, we never reached a trail that would've given us a solid family foundation. It was our prayer to rid China of cancer, and that was granted. We prayed daily for God to remove the toxic disease. *Be careful what you pray for!* Cancer hadn't been the only thing taken. God took her life as well.

When questioning His work, I asked, "Why me, Lord?"

I heard the voice respond, "Why not you?"

God tried to tell me something. In our relationship, I hadn't listened; I'd wanted to argue with Him. How senseless was that, knowing that I couldn't have won? China was only loaned to me; she was never mine to keep. The Lord giveth, and so shall He taketh.

It had taken an eternity to embrace His message. We must be humble and take heed when God speaks. There is a mighty and powerful force in all He does.

Our story is a way of helping others, a mission I have vowed to perform so others may know the wrath of toxic relationships. And they disguise themselves in many forms.

For me, the workplace became a toxic environment. Many have wondered how I could've stayed there those fourteen years after China's passing. Well, that's been a mystery to the doctors as well. One thing is for certain: it felt as though I'd been raped—physically, spiritually, and mentally. When I tell you I lost my freakin' mind, that's no joke. I'd literally gone bonkers. Whenever I give my word, in any situation, I'm true to that commitment. Perhaps that one personality trait was why I clung to such toxic emotions. At least, that's how I rationalized the degree of my anger and rage in relationships that I harbored throughout the years.

If you're curious about how I managed to leave the toxic work environment, it was the actions of those inner voices. We've all heard them at one time or another—perhaps not as dangerously, though. I couldn't help but listen. They were screaming to escape. To satisfy your curiosity, I shall briefly walk you through the unfolding of that day.

While I sat reading the daily emails on my computer, I began hearing the inner voices. I took the palm of my hand and tapped it against the side of my head. Still their words lingered. No matter how much I tried to turn off the voices, they wouldn't settle. They screamed out, "It's time to kill, f*ck 'em; screw 'em all; first, kill the b*tch! Why are you still here? They didn't care about you or your daughter. Kill 'em all now!" I heard the voices echo inside my head.

As my mind raced, I felt my pressure rising and my heart pounding. I continued to hear these eerie voices.

Before I realized it, I was spread out on a stretcher, strapped down, and screaming about what happened on November 3, 1992. I bawled it all out, from Emily's interference to China's death. The EMTs couldn't check my vital signs fast enough. After assessing my breathing, my racing pulse rate, and the surging blood pressure, they worked diligently to stabilize me.

The first-aid office contacted Dawn before transporting me to Northwestern Memorial Hospital. After arriving in the emergency room, my vital signs became more irregular. With my mind ripped to pieces, all I could do was lay there screaming about the occurrences of 1992. 'Cause once the rage is finally unmasked, it can explode, releasing all the toxicity of anger. As I babbled on and on, it was Dawn who briefed the nursing staff about the actual events of that day. With no other remedy left, I had to be hospitalized and heavily sedated. While I was still in a zoned-out state, Dawn pushed me in the wheelchair through the corridors. Reaching a floor, the elevator doors opened. Dawn suddenly looked up and saw an overhead sign whose main words read "Psychiatric."

As she placed her index finger to her lips, she quickly bent over, and in a vehement, loud whisper told me, "I want you to zip it! If you want to get out of here, don't mention another word about 1992!"

And I did as she told me. When doctors surrounded me at my bedside, I denied recalling any events of 1992. This totally puzzled them all, and they persistently poked around for the details. With the psycho drugs running through me, the doctors continuously tested my mental state for the next several days. But by the weekend, they discharged me. So after leaving the hospital, I never returned to the office where I had worked in Chicago. That work environment had become way too toxic. And the scars still remain.

After traveling on our journey, I hope that you've been inspired to take a stand, have been touched enough to share our story with others, and have been educated about the scope of toxic and nontoxic relationships.

Stand up and speak out, 'cause once attacked, there's no question where your shoe prints will lead or the effects that toxicity will bring. Our experiences with these types of toxic relationships have been a mystery.

Remember, our life is designed with no dress rehearsals. We get one chance to walk our journey, but no do-overs. So make it count—and live it to the fullest!

Well, thanks for walking the journey with me and being great listeners! I appreciate you staying until the end. It has been so therapeutic for me. Just know I've found peace and comfort. If there is a precious gift I can give others, it would be our story. And that's an accomplishment that will span generations.

The Insight

Where there is a relationship with grief, it's built on a formula:

Pain + Anger + Denial + Guilt + Depression + Hope = Grief

- When it comes to grieving, there is no right or wrong way.
- Grief is a felt pain and a personal emotion.

Feelings

Feelings are things inside that
make your body get a thrill
Or sometimes will just shiver you
into a cold chill
It's easy to identify these ills
since He has taken away my thrills

For twenty-one years, I'd gone through life
loved and needed
I'd woken one morn as He blessed
me with a young born
'Tis the happiest, joyous, and
cheeriest day of my life
She was something more than just right
Of course, I was like a kid with a new bike

Always selfish, protective, and ready to fight
Guess I've always wanted to hold on real tight

But, when I'd awoken another day
He'd called her to come His way
Now as I go on about my life
things just don't seem right
I've walked around in a maze
Looking to touch her with each phase
that's when I got cold waves
'Cause cold ills are not a good thrill
it's simply another type of chill.
Love always,

Mom

APPENDIX A

Support Vessels

Regardless of the toxic form, support is available throughout the healing journey. Whether for yourself or for someone you know, these are some resources for support:

A Safe Place
Embassy for Support
www.asafeplaceforhelp.org
800.854.3552

American Cancer Society
Embassy for Support
www.cancer.org
800.227.2345

Cancer Resource Centre
Programs Support Group
www.cancerresourcecentre.com
219.836.3349

Domestic Violence & Sexual Assault Services
Embassy for Support
www.dvsas.org
877.715.1563

Gilda's Club Chicago
Support Group and Kid's Program
www.gildasclubchicago.org
888.445.3248

Homestead Hospice
Programs Support Group
www.homesteadhospice.com
678.966.0077

Leukemia and Lymphoma Society
Informational and Support Groups
www.lls.org
800.955.4572

Mothers Supporting Daughters with Breast Cancer
Support Vehicle
www.mothersdaughters.org
410.778.1982

Rush Day Hospital
Support Programs
www.rush.edu
312.942.5375

Workplace Bullying Institute
Support Vehicle
www.workplacebullying.org
360.656.6630

Food for thought: No matter where our journeys lead, it's our shoe prints that dictate the destination.

APPENDIX B

Resource Centers

W hile maneuvering through emotional obstacles, there are entities to help fight toxic relationships and embrace care needs. These are a few such establishments:

Betty Ford Center
39000 Bob Hope Dr.
Rancho Mirage, CA 92270
www.bettyfordcenter.org
800.434.7365

Cancer Treatment Centers of America
At Midwestern Regional Medical Center
2520 Elisha Avenue
Zion, IL 60099
www.cancercenter.com/midwestern
888.899.9424

Cleveland Clinic Cancer Center
9500 Euclid Avenue
Cleveland, OH 44106
www.clevelandclinic.org
800.223.2273

Emory Transplant Center
1364 Clifton Road NE
Atlanta, GA 30322
www.transplant.emory.edu
800.753.6679

Four Circles Recovery Center
156 Clear Crossing Lane
Horse Shoe, NC 28742
www.fourcirclesrecovery.com
877.241.7670

Johns Hopkins Hospital
600 North Wolfe Street
Baltimore, MD 21287
www.hopkinskimmelcancercenter.org
410.276.8560

Lakeside Treatment Center
1240 US Highway 1
North Palm Beach, FL 33408
www.lakesidedrugrehab.com
877.494.8522

Massachusetts Transplant Center
55 Fruit Street
Boston, MA 02114
www.massgeneral.org
877.644.2860

Mayo Clinic
200 First Street SW
Rochester, MN 55905
www.mayoclinic.org/rochester
507.284.2511

Piedmont Cancer Center
1800 Howell Mill Road
Suite 750
Atlanta, GA 30318
www.piedmont.org
404.425.7925

Radiation Oncology Services
275 Professional Court, Suite A
Riverdale, GA 30274
www.radonc.com
770.994.1650

Saint Jude Medical Center
101 E. Valencia Mesa Dr.
Fullerton, CA 92835
www.stjudemedicalcenter.org
714.871.3280

Food for thought: There is no place in our lives for toxic relationships. Take an active role to turn a negative into a positive.

Awareness Ribbon Colors

Throughout our environment, toxicity attaches itself to us through many disguises: drugs, alcohols, diseases, people, and even battlefields. These elements of toxic relationships are often represented by an awareness ribbon. Interesting, huh? There's an array of ribbons in circulation that symbolize and share colors with certain causes, many of which deal with toxicity. This list will aid in recognizing some of them.

Black: victims of 9/11, melanoma, gang prevention

Black and light blue: loss of a brother, loss of a male child, mourning a brother or son

Black and pink: loss of sister, loss of female child, mourning a sister or daughter

Burgundy: cesarean section, headaches/migraines, hospice care, multiple myeloma

Cream: paralysis, spinal diseases

Dark blue: child abuse prevention, victim rights, hurricane support, free speech

Flag: victims and heroes of 9/11, patriotism and support the troops, fireworks safety

Gray: asthma, brain cancer/brain tumors, diabetes, borderline personality disorder

Green: bipolar, cerebral palsy, depression, kidney/ovarian cancer, missing children, mental health

Indigo: bullying, harassment, stalking

Jigsaw puzzle: autism, child-to-child care and development

Lace: osteoporosis

Lime green: lymphoma

Navy blue and orange: Batten disease

Orange: leukemia, lupus, Agent Orange exposure, humane treatment of animals

Pale yellow: spina bifida

Pearl, white, or clear: lung cancer/lung disease, multiple sclerosis

Pink: breast cancer, birth parents, childhood cancer

Purple: Alzheimer's, drug overdose, pancreatic cancer, cystic fibrosis, children with disabilities

Rainbow: gay pride and support, domestic abuse

Red: heart and stroke, HIV/AIDS (World AIDS Day), burn victim, substance abuse

Red, white, and blue: victims at Millard South High School (in Nebraska)

Silver: elder abuse, Parkinson's disease, children with physical or learning disabilities, stalking

Teal: ovarian, cervical, and uterine cancers, anti-bullying, post-traumatic stress disorder

Turquoise: addiction recovery, congenital diaphragmatic hernia

Violet: Hodgkin lymphoma

White: gay teen suicide, peace, right to life, Pope John Paul II—"Rest in Peace"

Yellow, black, and red: post-traumatic stress disorder, traumatic brain injury

Yellow: suicide prevention, bone cancer, amber alert, liver cancer, support the troops

Zebra print: rare disease

<hr>

Food for thought: Remember, we're all born to bear gifts. It's how we distribute our gifts that makes an impact.

Chain of Connection

A s a patient or caregiver you may feel isolated—you're not alone! In addition to the support services, there are a variety of books available. Whether the relationship has been with cancer or a post-traumatic stress disorder, here are some reading materials.

Materials on Cancer

After Cancer: A Guide to Your New Life by Wendy Schlessel Harpham: question and answer book that addresses a wide range of issues.

Alternatives in Cancer Therapy: The Complete Guide to Non-Traditional Treatments by Ross Pelton and Lee Overholser: offers help for patients coping with cancer.

Beating Cancer with Nutrition: Clinically Proven and Easy-to-Follow Strategies by Dr. Patrick Quillin: information to help patients' quality and quantity of life.

Cancer and Its Management by Robert Souhami and Jeffrey Tobias: an introductory text on the principles of diagnosis, staging, and treatment of tumors.

Cancer Cure: The Complete Guide to Finding and Getting the Best Care There Is by Gary L. Schine and Ellen B. Berlinsky: shows readers how to take charge of their illnesses, treatments, and recovery.

Cancer Schmancer by Fran Drescher: discloses her personal experiences with uterine cancer.

Cancer Talk by Selma Schimmel: the various cancer experiences shared by an array of people.

50 Essential Things to Do When the Doctor Says It's Cancer by Greg Anderson: offers fifty steps to help fight the disease.

Fight Now: Eat & Live Proactively Against Breast Cancer by Aaron Tabor: becoming proactive against breast cancer with specific food and lifestyle choices.

Sammy's Mommy Has Cancer by Sherry Kohlenbey: a mom's battle with breast cancer and the measures used to inform a child.

The Cancer Conqueror: An Incredible Journey to Wellness by Greg Anderson: how a positive attitude and a hopeful spirit affects cancer.

Materials on Post-Traumatic Stress Disorder

8 Keys to Safe Trauma Recovery by Babette Rothschild: gives skills to understanding and implementing eight keys to successful trauma healings.

Finding Life Beyond Trauma by Drs. Victoria Follette and Jacqueline Pistorello: based on acceptance and commitment therapy to heal from post-traumatic stress disorder problems.

Healing from Trauma: A Survivor's Guide to Understanding Your Symptoms & Reclaiming Your Life by Jasmin Lee Cori: helps to understand trauma and its devastating impacts.

Mind-Body Workbook for PTSD: A 10-week Program for Healing after Trauma by Stanley H. Block and Carolyn Bryant Block: self-guided bridging program you can complete in ten weeks.

Post-Traumatic Stress Disorder: The Victim's Guide to Healing & Recovery by Raymond B. Flannery Jr.: understanding the responses a person undergoes after an acute trauma experience.

The War at Home by Shawn J. Gourley: one family's fight against PTSD; book for military families coping with PTSD.

Thirty Days with My Father: Finding Peace from Wartime PTSD by Christal Presley: a daughter's journey dealing with her father's post-traumatic stress syndrome.

Walking the Tiger: Healing Trauma by Peter A. Levine and Ann Frederick: the symptoms of trauma and steps needed to heal them.

The Author: Then to Now

Have you ever said what you will never do? Well, never say never. This author has, and she has since retracted those words.

The author, Nina Norstrom, grew up in a small suburban town outside Chicago, Illinois. She received her bachelor's degree from Concordia University. Norstrom is a member of AuthorsDen, The Author's Club Blog, Goodreads, Bublish Authorpreneur, and the American Cancer Society Cancer Action Network, among others.

Norstrom began writing in 1992, but it wasn't until 2010 that she was able to publish *The Big C: A Weapon of Death*. There's a bit of history behind that.

"The hardest part was coming up with a title," she says. "Before it ever took form, other names were given. These were titles like *Triumph of a Trooper, Only Those Who Suffer Know, and You and I Against the World.*"

Several unsuccessful attempts were made to release the story, but the author never gave up—even when the rejection letters flowed in.

This second edition is another achievement. To her readers, she gives a word of advice: *never surrender your mission.*

Specifically to women, she states, "Many, many years ago, I jeopardized my integrity for a man. Don't ever do that! Integrity is what keeps one's character intact. Of course, my entire journey with toxic relationships has been an overwhelming experience. But, the most devastating one was the diseased relationship with cancer."

In the midst of their journey, Nina and her daughter went from church to church praying for God to spare her daughter's life. Staying all day, many times they worshipped among sanctified congregations, praising His glory.

As they clung to faith, her daughter asked, "Mommy, do you think God is going to take away my cancer now?"

Nina replied, "Yeah, I believe He is."

After her daughter's homecoming, the author admits she became alienated from her faith. Whether just or not, she harbored emotions of rage, guilt, and anger. She struggled with those toxic emotions. But realizing it wasn't the righteous place to be within her heart and spirit, she's grown tremendously and moved on to relinquish that internal state. And she is grateful those days of acting out are far behind.

Along this journey, there were times when just mentioning cancer caused her to cringe. Crippled by her grief and blinded by faith, she never found closure while holding onto her past. She has gone through numerous rounds of therapy. In one of those phases, she spent many, many years going back and forth between support groups. Her first group was The Centre for Living with Dying, in Palos Heights, Illinois. Later, that group's name was changed to The Centre for New Beginnings. This center offered an array of services for major life transitions.

Unfortunately, the author required more than just forums to grow into her healing relationships. During certain periods, she was hospitalized and participated in group and one-on-one sessions, all while clinging to a small circle of supporters. This healing period lasted from November 1992 to November 2011.

That was years of therapeutic work. But since everyone's grief relationship varies, it's Nina's belief that for others it may not take as long to maneuver through the healing process. For Nina, her grief was affected by the relationships with her daughter's father, with God, and with the toxic work environment.

"Truly, I wasn't surprised when Craig failed to attend the homecoming ceremony. I may never forget how he treated our daughter, but I've learned to forgive," she says. "It's that forgiveness phase that has allowed me to be in a better place within my healing process. And I've come to realize Craig alone must answer for his actions.

"While going through the suffering, I told God how angry I was with Him for putting me through that miserable hurting period. As if that wasn't enough, I told Him I'd never forgive him. But I came full circle. I felt the pain our Holy Father endured seeing His son crucified: the pain, the suffering, and all that hurt. It was then I realized it's what we must bear to find our way through life. I've learned to *never* say what you won't ever do.

"Now, as for the therapy and support relationships, they do work! Most importantly, the journaling. It was those mechanisms that actually helped release the negative energy I clung to about the job. Those traumatic events I had to let them go—too painful to remember. Without these tools in place, a transition to recovery would have been frozen. There are many of us who experience post-traumatic stress disorder relationships and are labeled as damaged goods. At my workplace, coworkers referred to me as *the Crazy Lady!* Be mindful when judging others, you never know the battles one has faced.

"But, the most important lesson to share is: if not for letting go of the past and regaining a spiritual relationship, I never would have found my way back.

"It's all been a learning experience. Being a parent is one of life's greatest challenges and pleasures. And I am grateful to have made it from where I've been to where I'm at in my journey—for every day has been a new *life*.

"In a sense, what's most rewarding is taking one's daughter (in spirit) and finding one's self in a new beginning!"

For five years, the author walked alongside a diseased relationship—and that has made her an advocate for fighting back. She continues to embrace her work with the American Cancer Society and Hospice Care. But it was not always like that: the supporters who traveled inside her circle can attest to how deeply her religious side was buried. Coming out of hurtful relationships and into life anew, it is through sharing her story that she was able to blossom.

She's come full circle.